UNNECESSARY WARS

HENRY REYNOLDS is one of Australia's best-known historians. His pioneering scholarly work has included *The Other Side of the Frontier* (1981), *The Law of the Land* (1987), *This Whispering in Our Hearts* (1998) and *Why Weren't We Told?* (1999). His most recent book, *Forgotten War*, won the Victorian Premier's Literary Award for Non-fiction in 2014.

UNNECESSARY WARS

HENRY REYNOLDS

NEWSOUTH

A NewSouth book

Published by
NewSouth Publishing
University of New South Wales Press Ltd
University of New South Wales
Sydney NSW 2052
AUSTRALIA
newsouthpublishing.com

First published 2016

10 9 8 7 6 5 4 3 2 1

National Library of Australia Cataloguing-in-Publication entry
Creator: Reynolds, Henry, 1938– author.
Title: Unnecessary wars / Henry Reynolds.
ISBN: 9781742234809 (paperback)
9781742242279 (ebook)
9781742247649 (ePDF)
Subjects: South African War, 1899–1902 – Social aspects.
War and society – Australia.
Militarization – Australia.
Dewey Number: 303.660994

Design Josephine Pajor-Markus
Cover design Xou Creative
Cover image Vintage colour lithograph of the Second Boer War, South Africa, 1900. iStock.com/unknown artist.
Printed and bound by CPI Group (UK) Ltd, Croydon, CR0 4YY

This book is printed on paper using fibre supplied from plantation or sustainably managed forests.

UNSW
AUSTRALIA

Contents

And yet I doubt if there be a more reprehensible human act than to lead a nation into an unnecessary war …

Richard Cobden to John Bright, 8 August 1855[1]

Whoever knows what war really is, whoever will reflect upon its terrible effects and disastrous consequences, will readily agree that it should not be undertaken without the most urgent reasons for doing so. Humanity revolts against a sovereign who, without necessity or without pressing reasons, wastes the blood of his most faithful subjects and exposes his people to the calamities of war, when he could have kept them in the enjoyment of an honorable and salutary peace. When to this inconsiderateness, this want of love for his people, he adds the injustice towards those whom he attacks, of what crime, or rather of what dreadful series of crimes, does he not render himself guilty? Answerable for all the evils which he inflicts upon his subjects, he is responsible also for all those which he inflicts upon an innocent people – the bloodshed, the pillaging of towns, the ruin of provinces – such are his crimes. Not a man is killed nor a hut burned but he is responsible before God and answerable to humanity for them.

Emmerich de Vattel, The Law of Nations, *1758*[2]

Introduction

Why write another book about war? And why focus on the Boer War in particular? They are fair questions. The number of war books has increased dramatically over the last few years. Do we need any more? Obviously I decided that we do, but I did not seek to emulate the many studies of tactics and battles, soldiers and their commanders. Australia has numerous good professional military historians and an even greater number of enthusiastic amateurs. They have explored most of the country's campaigns and examined the careers of many distinguished soldiers.

I am not a military historian in the conventional sense of that term. I make no attempt to match those writers who chronicle battles and campaigns. I cannot compete with competent specialisation. Rather, my concern is with the broader question of the place of war in Australian society. This in turn is a response to the rhetoric that has proliferated during the current extended season of commemoration, which has reached a new intensity with the centenary of the First World War. I find it provokes many troubling thoughts. Why is Australia spending more money commemorating the First World War than any comparable country?[1] Why are we more obsessed with war than is New Zealand, for instance? And it is not just a response to the centenary of Anzac and the Western Front. The cavalcade of commemoration has been on the road for twenty years. For someone of my generation, watching it pass by has been an unexpected experience, and I wonder why that is so. Consideration of the question carries me back to my childhood. I have no recollection of the rhetorical flourishes common today. I suppose we must have had Anzac Day ceremonies at school but I remember very little about them, which suggest to me that the students as a whole had no particular interest in the proceedings. And I wonder if the teachers themselves were all that engaged in the process. I don't remember anyone inspiring us with the famous story of the dawn assault at Gallipoli.

When as a young adult I came to study and then to teach Australian history, the overseas war was well down my list of important topics. I took my cue from that generation of historians who, in the middle years of the 20th century, pioneered both the teaching and the writing of our national story. They were men and women who had lived through the Second World War. Many of them had served in one way or another, and to do so had put their careers on hold. The whole emphasis of the histories they wrote was on nation-building and on political and social development. They focused on domestic achievements, not on overseas military adventures. Australia was homemade by men and women who built and nurtured, who saved and taught. It was as if the actual experience of conflict had provided them with a protective shield against the excesses of military bravado.

One event in particular roused both my interest and concern about the current apotheosis of the soldier. In May 2013, I attended a public ceremony in Hobart on the edge of the large area of bushland on a hill known as the Queens Domain. It was a commemoration of Tasmania's involvement in the Boer War and was attended by an array of official representatives – mayors of local municipalities, state politicians or their representatives, a municipal band, and a party of horsemen dressed in the uniforms similar to those worn out on the veldt in the first months of the 20th century. I was surprised that after all this time Tasmanians were coming together to remember an almost forgotten war. The monument that was the focal point for the ceremony had a soldier standing on a plinth looking down on the city. It had been there since a few years after the war. In all the innumerable times I had walked or driven past it, I had never seen anyone bothering to pay tribute or show any interest in his lonely vigil. My father was a devoted historian who had an expansive curiosity about Tasmanian history and would constantly talk about past events and significant localities. He never once bothered to explain to me who the lonely soldier was or why he was there, although he would have known. It just did not seem to be important. And that was a common attitude. Why the renewed interest, I wondered, after a hundred years of neglect?

But as I thought about the ceremony I had seen, I concluded that the Boer War *should* be remembered, though not in the way I had witnessed. Commemoration of the service and sacrifice of the individual soldiers hinders rather than assists our attempt to understand the war itself. It deflects attention away from questions that still matter. And if that is true of the Boer War it is likely to be true about later conflicts. But the war in South Africa involved all six individual Australian colonies. For each one, apart from New South Wales, it was their first war. It was also an unnecessary one. And the new federal government inherited a role in the conflict in 1901 without any doubt or regret, and was involved in it for the first seventeen months of its existence.

The politicians who made the decision for war in the seven parliaments and fourteen chambers engaged in the most sustained conversation about war and peace, about nation and empire, in Australian history. The questions articulated and the doubts intimated in those debates are still of interest. Why did Australia go so readily to war? Why did the colonies overthrow an implicit tradition of non-involvement in Britain's imperial wars? And why go to a war fought half a world away in the remote interior of Africa against people who could never present a threat to the Australian continent? Was the sacrifice of 600 young lives worthwhile? Had a fateful precedent been established? Did anything of lasting value accrue to the new Federation? Did anyone bother to count the cost in lives and treasure?

Many of the dissidents also voiced the concern that the new Federation, while conceived in peace, was born in war. By 1902, after a conflict lasting two years and seven months, there was already much talk about the Australian contingents displaying distinctive colonial characteristics – Australia had entered into its long love affair with the warrior. And other related traditions had already emerged. In speeches in parliaments and before public meetings and patriotic rallies, important men declared that as a result of the war Australia had come of age, had become a nation. War was welcomed as an inimitable rite of passage.

The war and Federation were contemporaneous. Many of the so-called founding fathers who were instrumental in the campaign for federal union – who had attended the great conventions to draft the Constitution and campaigned for the cause in the following referendums – were strong supporters of the commitment to war. They seem to have felt no sense of contradiction between the two ventures. But this was often the point of greatest anguish for the opponents of war. Australia's hitherto peaceful nation-building was, they believed, diametrically opposed to foreign military entanglements, which were a betrayal of what the new nation stood for. And there was more to it than that. The spirit of militarism born of the involvement was antithetical to the great democratic achievements of colonial Australia and might in the long run prove more enduring.

The Boer War was, then, as much of a landmark as was Federation, although often not recognised as such. Both dealt with questions that had been considered since the middle of the 19th century. Federation resolved the problem of the relationship between the individual colonies. The Constitution was a detailed plan dividing power between the two levels of government, but it did little to change the relationship between Australia and the imperial government. The war, on the other hand, resolved a number of what had been enduring questions about the colonies' reaction to Britain's wars. Were they necessarily involved? Was there a responsibility to become engaged anywhere at any time? Was neutrality a possible, even a desirable stance? Should Australia concentrate on defence of the continent or follow Britain into overseas conflicts on the assumption that such engagement would guarantee future protection?

There are, then, two enduring legacies of decisions made at the turn of the 20th century: the federal compact and the involvement in overseas wars. It is still not clear which will have the most decisive or enduring impact on our national life. The habit of going off to war may prove even harder to change than the wording of the Constitution.

In this book we will examine Australia's history of debate about war and peace, nation and empire, and how the Boer War set in train habits of thought and action we now take for granted. We might begin our investigation by considering Australia's involvement in unnecessary wars and how they have been commonly regarded and remembered.

1

Unnecessary wars

As I write this, we are in the middle months of 2015 and Australia is again at war. Or it might be more correct to say Australia is still at war. Since 2001 we have been continuously involved in the Middle East, and the current government seems to have no clear idea as to when this commitment will come to an end. The retired former head of the Australian army, Professor Peter Leahy, recently declared that we are now 'involved in the early stages of a war which is likely to last for the rest of the century'.[1] While that may appear alarmist, Australia's involvement in war in the 20th century should give us pause for thought. For during the seventy-six years since the outbreak of the Second World War in 1939, the country has been involved in war for fifty-eight years, or more than three-quarters of that time, although this includes the occupation of Japan between the end of the war and the signing of the Peace Treaty in 1951. It has clearly become more common than not for Australia to be involved in conflict somewhere in the world. Has war become more normal for us than peace? Are we now in a situation where governments not only do not seek to avoid military interventions overseas but positively court them and suffer no consequential political pain?

Meanwhile, for the last twenty years the community has been engaged in a swelling cavalcade of commemoration to mark the centenary of the First World War and of the Anzac landing of 1915 in particular. Generous government funding has promoted the publication of books, the making of documentaries, the creation of sophisticated curriculum material for schools. Old monuments have been restored all over the country and new ones erected. Re-enactments, large and small, are well funded. Scholarships and prizes have been awarded to allow schoolchildren to tour battlefields in Europe and the Middle East. Service records are now available on the internet, enabling families to trace the military careers of hitherto little known or long forgotten ancestors.

The key message promoted by government instrumentalities – the Department of Veterans' Affairs and the Australian War Memorial in particular – is that war has been the central and the defining national experience. At the heart of this militarisation of national history remains the Gallipoli campaign, which, countless voices insist, created the nation and defined what it means to be Australian. This message became more deeply entrenched during the ceremonies held on and around Anzac Day 2015, the centenary of the landing.

But there is something both strange and partial about this crescendo of commemoration. The whole emphasis is on the service, achievements and sacrifice of individuals. The contemporary fusion of military and family history intensifies the focus to such an extent that battles, campaigns, even enemies and wars, become undifferentiated. They collectively provide the occasion and the location for the display of Australian character and martial virtue. So, rather than create the space for searching questions about our long history of overseas military involvement, the emphasis on individual valour and sacrifice crowds out the whole field. Commemoration is not the same as consideration, and may be the enemy of analysis. To ask the big questions about war is seen to take attention away from the heroism and suffering of many thousands of servicemen now increasingly claimed by proprietorial descendants. So the more we talk about war, the less able we are to cast a sceptical eye, let alone a critical one, on the nation's military history. As a result many questions go begging.

To begin with, it would be a good start to interrogate the current semi-official assertion that war has been the defining national experience. If we look from the opposite direction, the big question is why has Australia been involved in so many wars in so many parts of the world? This makes Australia quite exceptional among small and medium-sized powers, many of which have sought to avoid wars whenever they could. Is Australia, then, uniquely warlike, inimitably belligerent? And there is the strange paradox that Australians have always deeply resented any interference by foreigners in our internal affairs while being ever ready to intervene in countries far away. It might help to think more clearly about our war history to consider what the world would have been like if all the many other similar-sized powers had sent their armed forces off in all directions as regularly as we have done since the Sudan expedition in 1885. During the 20th century Australia has behaved less like a normal nation-state and more like the handmaiden of the great powers – as a pint-sized imperialist. We have found it difficult to differentiate between our own national interest and those of our two great and powerful friends.

There is as well a need to question whether our institutions clear the path to war. Does the unfettered power accorded the Crown – and in effect the executive – to decide on questions of war and peace make military engagement more rather than less likely? Australian governments can go to war without the sanction of parliament, even without seeking a supporting debate. Does the continuous commemoration of past wars make it easier to become involved in new ones? Is war thereby normalised? Does the fact that Australia has had very little direct experience of war – apart from the destruction in 1942 of what was then a very remote Darwin – allow the country to indulge in a mood of insouciance about armed conflict? Never having seen our own land devastated, we seem unable to empathise with those peoples who have. And we assume we have the moral right to fight wherever we choose, often far away from our homeland. Despite a crowded history of conflict, Australians have not often had debates about the morality of war itself or felt any pressing need to discuss the niceties of international law. Another striking characteristic of Australia's attitude to war is that the country has rarely given retrospective consideration to the question of whether our wars were essential to our safety and well-being, if the commitment of life and treasure was worthwhile, and what if anything was actually gained. Alone among government activities, war escapes actuarial scrutiny.

Another distinctive feature of Australian war history is that many of our involvements have been in countries we knew very little about, places contemporaries would not have been able to find easily on a map. And the wars were often wholly or in part civil wars, the complexities of which passed the Australians by. And even more obvious is the fact that practically all the enemies engaged by Australian troops presented no threat to the country and never could in any realistic assessment of future dangers. This robbed Australia of the most common and pressing justification for war, embedded in international law for centuries: the danger of an imminent threat of attack. Such concerns rarely seem to enter into the national reflection on past conflict.

As a result, our current season of commemoration is constricted by an outlook that is essentially amoral and narrowly nationalistic. By concentrating on the service, suffering and sacrifice of our own personnel, we give almost no attention to the devastation we have caused in many places around the world. We carefully count every fallen Australian. We show little interest in – or concern, it seems – for the enemy killed, the fathers who left widows and children behind, the families devastated, the lifelong grief occasioned by Australian troops. Our empathy and compassion is closely contained, focused on those who wore our own uniforms. The constant emphasis on our military prowess is never brought down to where it must ultimately rest: on the capacity our young men have shown to be efficient killers.

The one place where the consequences of conflict are unavoidable is the enduring frontier fighting between settlers and Aboriginal people. But that has never officially been considered as warfare and so can be deftly avoided by keeping our eyes closely focused on fighting beyond our borders. But much remains to be said. Fighting here and fighting over there were contemporaneous. In 1885, when New South Wales sent a contingent of 700 men to war in the Sudan, there was intense conflict right across northern Australia. It continued while all the colonies sent troops to South Africa and was still apparent in remote areas of the continent after the Great War. Did it have any effect on the thinking of Australians about the empire and their place in the world? It is an interesting albeit rarely considered question, but certain relevant matters can be canvassed. Among the men who shaped the Constitution, committed troops to war in South Africa and entered the new federal parliament, many had been in public life for a generation. The leaders of Queensland, South Australia and Western Australia, in particular, would all have been aware of the persistent fighting in the tropical north and the central deserts, which was the subject of newspaper articles, official reports and parliamentary debates. It was common in the late 19th century to relate this domestic conflict to Britain's many other colonial wars. The Australian frontier, it was often thought, was one part of the much larger, more widespread imperial frontier. The pioneers were extending the reach, not just of their particular colony, but of the empire as well. And the leaders of the time were convinced that force was legitimate both to secure the continent and then to hold it as the exclusive domain of the 'white race'. This was their implicit foreign policy, their own imperial project. Colonial hostility to resulting criticism from humanitarians in Britain added fuel to a more general rejection of that important strain of liberalism associated with the so-called Manchester School of Richard Cobden, John Bright and William Gladstone. Moral concern in Britain was seen to be insufferable interference in Australian affairs. The colonists were carried comfortably along in the late 19th-century intellectual currents that led onwards and upwards to the apotheosis of imperialism.

Colonial life encouraged the growth of a sense of racial superiority. It seemed to confirm social Darwinism and the attendant operation of what were locally called the iron laws of evolution. The Aboriginal people were almost universally thought to be a dying race. The ascendant Anglo-Saxons were destined to dominate the world. The empire was both a manifestation of racial predominance and the instrument for its political realisation. Racial thinking spread more widely and penetrated more deeply in Australia than in Britain. It pervaded thought about, and the policies that were shaped to deal with, Indigenous Australians. It dominated attitudes to the Asian diaspora in the colonies and the debate about Australia's anomalous place as a British enclave in an Asian sphere. Many Australians came to believe that racial affinity drew them to the empire. The blood tie was both visceral and irresistible. The same forces produced a latent racial hostility that, it was thought, would eventually lead to conflict between Australia and Japan. Race complicated Australian thinking about our place in the world, making it difficult to develop realistic attitudes towards or pragmatic policies about either Britain or Japan.

There is another distinctive feature of Australia's war history. Our geographical situation has meant that our wars and campaigns have usually been located a long way away. We had no land borders to defend, no threatening next-door neighbours, no ancestral enemies. The surrounding seas were an immediate challenge to would-be invaders, and the sheer size of the continent provided another. This brings us to one of the central paradoxes of Australian history: the very circumstances that could have kept us out of war actually had the reverse effect. Lacking any contiguous challenge, the country felt sufficiently secure to send large armies overseas, leaving the homeland vulnerable. Only in 1942 did the strategy leave us on the brink of disaster.

Australia has exhibited little interest in the different strategic decisions of those countries that have used their particular location and distinctive traditions to avoid rather than fight wars. We never showed any attraction to the strategy of the many republics of Latin America to avoid direct involvement in European wars. Nor have we had much sympathy for the smaller European countries that have remained neutral – Norway, Sweden, Denmark, the Netherlands, Switzerland and Spain in the First World War; Sweden, Switzerland, Ireland, Portugal and Spain in the Second. In discussion about the First World War, Australian audiences are quite surprised to hear that European countries so close to the conflict chose not to go to war in 1914 whereas Australia plunged in from the first day of conflict. Every now and then the idea of neutrality has been debated, but it has gained little traction. At various times, prominent Australians have called for a radical reassessment of the traditional policy of military intervention, and they do so again today. The major political parties have shrunk from any such venture and still avoid the question. It means that the momentous question remains unasked and, consequently, unanswered. Has Australia been involved in many unnecessary wars it could have avoided? Would we have been much better off if we had eschewed rather than courted war? Has our tradition of overseas military engagement, now intensely commemorated, been a terrible, profound and continuing mistake? Did the large-scale sacrifice achieve anything commensurate with the loss of life, the prodigal waste of resources? Did generations of national leaders waste it all for little gain? Have Australian lives been constantly undervalued?

Any assessment of these questions must begin with the observation that Australia has, without exception, fought beside either Britain or the United States. They decided where and when we would be engaged, and who and why and in what manner we would fight. Australia, it is true, normally had its own reasons for becoming involved. Our political and military leaders decided that participation was in our national interest as perceived at the time. But the wars were always what are commonly and fairly referred to as other people's wars. The grand strategic decisions were made in London or Washington. So, too, were considered the other big questions involving political rationale, international law and public morality. With so much decided elsewhere, all that was left to Australia was to fight. Our two patrons chose our enemies and provided us with both weapons and the justification for using them. There was always a difficulty deciding if and when Australian national interest differed from that of our two great and powerful friends. The great gap in size and power that always existed between Australia and Britain and even more starkly between Australia and the United States meant that we were more a dependent than an ally in the normal meaning of that word. Constant talk about kinship disguised the demeaning status of a deferential and biddable client.

These matters have been woven into Australian experience since the late 19th century. The colonial and then federal leaders came to several portentous, interlocking and mutually supportive decisions whose consequences are still with us. The first was that Australia's geography was a source of danger. The isolation and size of the continent were widely seen as liabilities rather than strategic advantages. The resulting sense of insecurity led on to the second grand assumption: safety was assured by membership of the British Empire – the closer the relationship the better, promising future protection. The strategic interests of the empire, even its prestige, automatically involved Australia. Britain's enemies were Australia's enemies, her wars ours as well.

There were dissident voices that challenged these assumptions, arguing that proximity to the empire carried its own risks and would inevitably drag Australia needlessly into wars, whereas the isolation of the continent could allow for neutrality or at least non-intervention. The empire itself was a potent source of danger. Security would come from remaining at home and using the armed forces purely for defence of the homeland. The continent, not the empire, had to be the main concern of all international relations. Australian interests could be distinguished from those of Britain and should be given priority.

History has not dealt kindly with the small bands of republicans and nationalists who proposed this radically different future for Australia's international relations, and they have largely been forgotten. Their advocacy, prominent during the second half of the 19th century, was swamped when the governments of all the Australian colonies sent troops to the Boer War in 1899 and were widely applauded for so doing. The empire loyalists carried all before them, but in retrospect the dissidents promoted arguments that are still relevant today. Their enduring cogency has not been determined by community support at any particular moment, and their foreboding about the danger inherent in the imperial ties has been fully borne out. The burden of empire was a heavy one. Australia lost far more as a result than she gained during the first half of the 20th century. If, as we can now see, the First World War was disastrous for Europe, it was even more so for Australia because it was avoidable. The loss of 60 000 young men, the wounding of so many more, let alone the financial burden both during and after the war, were terrible consequences of imperial loyalty, partially foreseen by the dissidents. Australia's future security would have been more assured if all those young men had remained at home, as the dissidents wanted, and engaged their energies in raising families and developing the country. The vast expenditure could have been profitably invested here. Perhaps more to the point, the country would have had another couple of decades to develop the capacity to defend the continent itself and develop distinctive Australian strategic and defence policies.

But the great loss of life twisted the bonds of empire even tighter. How could a cause be questioned when so much had been given in its name? It had the irresistible sanction of sacrificial blood. The contemporary commemoration of the war makes it difficult even now to ask the really hard questions. What did Australia gain from the war that is in any way commensurate with such loss and devastation? And even when attempts are made to promote positive outcomes they are often exaggerated or even illusory. One only has to ask the question of what the country would have thought in 1914 to be worth the lives of so many young men. The Australians lost far more men fighting for the empire than the American colonists did fighting to gain their independence. But the Americans can look back and commemorate the war that led to the founding of the great republic. The Australians died for an empire that ceased to exist a little more than a generation after the signing of the Treaty of Versailles, when the last of the old diggers were still alive.

Mainstream Australia paid little attention at the time of Federation to the radicals who warned about the perils inherent in the apparently protective imperial embrace. They showed no more interest after the First World War. They were unable to learn the most obvious lesson about the burden of empire. They continued to place their faith in the empire after 1918. They expected that Mother England would be there when she was needed. They accepted the strategic plans that depended on the fortress island of Singapore and on the battle fleet that never arrived. As a result, 15 000 Australians were captured by the Japanese in 1942 while the bulk of our army and navy was on the other side of the world. And those decisions reverberate today. The country sought the same kind of relationship with the United States after the Second World War. How closely the patterns replicate! Australia went to war in Vietnam, Afghanistan and Iraq as a consequence of this relationship. They were countries we knew little about. None of them could possibly have presented a threat to the continent. We fought in places, at times and against enemies chosen for us. Our abiding insecurity led us to stand as close to the United States as we could, assuming that was the safest place to be.

The same dissident voices recur after more than a century, warning us of the danger of Australia's tradition of deference. Recently, ex-Liberal prime minister the late

Malcolm Fraser warned us that America was 'Australia's dangerous ally', arguing quite bluntly that:

> It is time for Australia to end its strategic dependence on the United States. The relationship with America, which has long been regarded as beneficial, has now become dangerous to Australia's future. We have effectively ceded to America the ability to decide when Australia goes to war. Even if America were the most perfect and benign power, this posture would still be incompatible with the integrity of Australia as a sovereign nation. It entails not simply deference but submission to Washington, an intolerable state of affairs for a country whose power and prosperity are increasing and whose national interests dictate that it enjoy amicable, not hostile, relations with its neighbors, including China … at the moment, because of U.S. military installations in Australia, if America goes to war in the Pacific, it will take us to war as well – without an independent decision by Australia.[2]

Some people expressed remarkably similar fears in the late 19th century, although their anxiety concerned Australia's close and deferential relationship with Britain rather than the United States. They believed that Britain would inevitably draw Australia into unnecessary wars that could be avoided. Fraser himself may not have been aware of the extent to which the roots of our present predicament reach back into our colonial past – that the habits of dependence are so ingrained, that Australia has still not escaped the smothering embrace of empire. If we seek understanding, we must revisit the past.

We might begin our exploration by considering how Australia celebrated the establishment of the Federation on 1 January 1901, then move on to a more detailed examination of Australia's role in the Boer War, and in the process examine the competing claims of empire and nation and many other matters as well.

2

Australia's first birthday

The first of January 1901, the opening day of the 20th century, was an important moment in many parts of the world, but nowhere more so than in Australia, with the inauguration of the new federal government. In towns and villages all over the continent, traditional New Year celebrations were enhanced by allusions to the birth of the Commonwealth. There were the ubiquitous picnics, marches, concerts and sports carnivals. Much attention was devoted to the children, the native-born citizens of the future. They marched behind local brass bands; gathered on sports grounds; were given lollies, cordial and cakes; and heard speeches from town councillors, members of parliament and earnest clergymen.

There was some uncertainty about how to commemorate the new nation, what flags should be flown, which events should be dedicated to its birth. There was confusion about whether the new Commonwealth or the old empire should take precedence. Many observers noted that the celebrations lacked the glamour that had surrounded those of April 1897 for Queen Victoria's Diamond Jubilee and the wild enthusiasm of 1899 when news came through about the lifting of the Boer sieges of Ladysmith and Mafeking (see chapter 7). The editor of the *Rockhampton Bulletin* thought the local celebrations very much resembled those marking the Diamond Jubilee, 'but they did not approach in their magnitude or excellence the display that was made on that occasion'.[1] The Hobart *Mercury* believed that many people, though enthusiastic at heart about Federation, were not sure how to 'decorate suitably' – the occasion was not patriotic in the way that the Boer War celebrations had been and 'it did not seem that the Union Jack could be aptly used again as the keynote of effect … Nor could the patriotic mottoes be set out again appropriately'.[2]

There were more formal events in each of the colonial, now state capitals. The governors addressed gatherings of politicians, judges, army officers and bureaucrats, and read the official proclamation establishing the Commonwealth. But many of the leading public figures from all over Australia had gathered in Sydney for a week of processions, banquets, concerts and conferences. Intercolonial rivalries were put aside and great festive crowds welcomed the birth of the nation. It was agreed that Sydney was the ideal place for the new Federation to be presented to the world.

The torrent of congratulatory speeches was reported in detail by correspondents in all the major national newspapers. Metaphors abounded; hyperbole flourished. The editor of the *Kalgoorlie Miner* declared that it was 'a red-letter day – a day such as she [Australia] can never see again – a day that will influence her destinies … for all time to come'. At the bidding of her people 'the Australian colonies did yesterday weld themselves into one, and take upon themselves the honours and the responsibilities of nationhood'.[3] The Launceston *Examiner* observed that the ceremonies in Sydney 'welded Australia into a nation – made her sons and daughters henceforth one people, with one destiny'.[4]

The pride was unmistakable and quite understandable. There was much to be admired. Late 19th-century Australia was a remarkably successful society. It seemed so at the time and it does now in retrospect. Australia and New Zealand had the highest global per capita income, and wealth was more evenly distributed than in most comparable societies. The literacy rate was among the highest in the world and universities had been established in Melbourne, Sydney, Adelaide and Hobart. The courts, parliaments and bureaucracies worked effectively with less corruption than in many other countries. Manhood suffrage had been in force in the major colonies for many years. Votes for women had been introduced in South Australia and Western Australia and were pending elsewhere and, most significantly, in the new federal system. Precocious trade union development had stalled in the depressed 1890s, but by 1900 organised labour had successfully forced its way into most of the colonial parliaments and was to hold the balance of power after the first federal elections in March 1901. The federal Constitution had been openly debated in a series of national conventions and had been put to the people in two referendums in Victoria, New South Wales, South Australia and Tasmania, and one each in Queensland and Western Australia. The document blended the traditions and customs that had emerged from the experience of the six colonial parliaments with elements of the federal system of the United States. The referendum was adopted from Switzerland. The selective borrowing notwithstanding, the Constitution was above all a homegrown product representing a decisive break from British constitutional practice. It was a significant political achievement.

The five eastern Australian colonies had been granted their own parliaments between 1856 and 1859 by an imperial government still dominated by the hereditary aristocracy. Only one-fifth of adult men in Britain had the vote. The colonies adopted the basic constitutional structures and well-entrenched parliamentary procedures from Westminster but moved rapidly to democratise political life a generation or more before comparable changes took place in Britain. In almost every advance towards full democracy, the Australian colonies led the way. The assertion that Australia adopted the 'Westminster system', as common in 1901 as it is today, totally distorts the relationship between the imperial parliament and the Australian legislatures. But overriding power still resided in Westminster in 1900. The Australian Constitution, although sanctioned by popular vote, still required the agreement of the British government and was embodied in an act of the imperial parliament. A popular expression at the time was that Federation had created a nation for a continent and a continent for a nation. The rhetoric did not quite meet the reality. The new national parliament did not have the full powers of a nation-state. External sovereignty was retained by the imperial government. Australia had only one foot on the edge of the international stage. The new federal parliament had little more power than those granted to the colonial legislatures more than forty years before.

In terms of its place in the world, the Australian Federation was still a colony rather than a sovereign state. And internally the new government did not exercise effective control over significant areas of the great land mass or the Indigenous communities that lived there. Large numbers of Aboriginal people were beyond the reach of government. In parts of Cape York, Arnhem Land, the Kimberley and the vast central deserts there were thousands of men, women and children who had never seen a white man. They were neither governed nor protected by the Australian state. Frontier warfare persisted in many parts of the north, although not referred to in any of the speeches delivered during the federal festivities. But memories were still fresh in rural New South Wales of the fear evoked by the murderous rampage of Jimmy and Joe Governor, called the 'Breelong Blacks', during the winter and spring of 1900. While Sydney celebrated, Jimmy Governor waited on death row in the prison in Darlinghurst. He was finally hanged on 18 January.

The absence of any references to Aboriginal Australia during the torrent of speeches in the first week of 1901 was only one of what, in retrospect, appear to be strange anomalies. The establishment of Federation and the creation of the Constitution capped several generations of creative political development paralleled by comparable social and economic progress. They were the cumulative achievements of several generations of colonists and increasingly of Australian-born men and women. While they often looked overseas for guidance, the emergent institutions, enterprises and manners were distinctly Australian. But in all the public events that were held to mark the first weeks of the new Federation, the inimitable local achievements were upstaged by the frisson and excitement of war and the glamour and well-rehearsed grandeur of the empire in what turned out to be the last weeks of Victoria's epic reign. Earnest, sedately dressed and often unknown colonial politicians were no match for swashbuckling soldiers returned from the veldt or visiting imperial regiments sporting gaudy multicoloured uniforms. The slow, cumulative colonial achievements, the complex Constitution, the unspectacular pioneering were hard to promote or to illustrate in engaging public display.

The great communal occasions in Sydney in that first week of the year can tell us much about the public mood. The opening event was a mass procession from Circular Quay to Centennial Park for the reading of the royal proclamation. Marching trade unionists and members of friendly societies received what the *Sydney Morning Herald* termed 'modest encouragement'. The intercolonial politicians who had been involved in the federal movement and the constitutional conventions were unknown to the crowds and met with only scattered clapping. Local politicians George Reid and Edmund Barton were recognised and applauded. But when the carriage of the new governor-general, the ceremonially attired seventh Earl of Hopetoun, appeared, 'the enthusiasm was limitless, and was renewed again and again'. The only competing attraction for the crowd's enthusiasm was the large contingent of British and Indian troops. In a move of calculated brilliance, the imperial government had sent more than 1000 representatives of six cavalry regiments, four artillery detachments and almost 500 members of nineteen of the most famous infantry regiments. The *Herald* reporter was caught up in the crowd's enthusiasm, describing how,

> the glittering cavalcade of Imperial troops swept by in stately majesty. Admirable, picturesque, magnificent, were the ejaculations one heard on all sides. Contingent after contingent came along the appointed route, each splendidly uniformed, and mounted on prancing steeds. Glittering swords and helmets flashed in the sunshine, sabres and spurs clanked, and plumes nodded. What waving of handkerchiefs there were, and how the multitude cheered.[5]

Military spectacle did not end with the street parade of 1 January. Even grander in the minds of the public was the military review held on Thursday, 3 January in Centennial Park. Ten thousand troops paraded before the governor-general, watched by a crowd estimated to be between 125 000 and 150 000. The correspondent writing for Brisbane's *Courier* observed that the enthusiasm of the vast crowd showed how popular the armed services were in the new Federation. He went on to note that

> it used to be popular to speak slightingly of the military forces, but the prowess of the British arms in South Africa, and the display of the natural fighting ability of our Australian soldiers, have given the army such a strong hold in the hearts of the people that it is now one of the most, if not the most, cherished idols among the deities of the populace. More than ever the Queen's uniform is irresistibly attractive, even to staid, sober citizens.[6]

There were a few references to peace during the celebrations in Sydney. As the governor-general's carriage paused beside St Mary's Catholic Cathedral, a choir of schoolchildren sang an ode concluding with the question:

> *What does the future hold*
> *For the land of the Golden Fleece?*
> *Lord, in Whose hands the Nations lie,*
> *Lord, let Thy gift be Peace!*

Later, in a prayer for the new Commonwealth, Cardinal Patrick Moran renewed the reference to peace. Australia, he announced, 'in the freshness of freedom and the vigour of youth … sets out on her peaceful career of Empire'. In one hand, he hoped, it would 'ever wield the sceptre of Christian civilisation' and in the other 'firmly grasp the gospel of peace'. He hoped that the 'crowning mission' of the Commonwealth would be to erect 'a glorious temple of abiding concord and long-enduring peace'.[7]

But peace did not stand a chance in the new Commonwealth. Each of the six colonies had sent troops to fight in South Africa. While the premiers were still in Sydney for the inauguration of the Commonwealth, they met and agreed to send new contingents to the war totalling 2500 men, along with their horses. Reporting the decision, the *Sydney Morning Herald* declared:

> We accept the request of the Imperial authorities for more Australian troops as a distinct compliment. It adds an official acknowledgement to those we have already received respecting the real merits of our men. It proves beyond cavil that they have won a reputation as soldiers of the Queen, and it amounts to a generous admission of the value of our contingents and their services.[8]

But as well as the war in South Africa, Australians were involved at the time of Federation in the international campaign to repress the Boxer Rebellion in China. Victoria, New South Wales and South Australia had sent a combined naval force of 500 men that saw little action. South Australia had dispatched its gunboat the *Protector*, which arrived back in Adelaide at the end of the first week of January. The crew were welcomed back as heroes by admiring crowds. They looked bronzed after the voyage, 'were in high spirits and pleased at the hearty welcome they received on all sides'. Reporting the return of the ship, the Adelaide *Advertiser* observed that the men considered themselves unfortunate

> in not having had an opportunity of fighting their ship, or of taking a share in any hostile demonstration on shore, but their inactivity in these directions arose from the pusillanimity of the Chinese and not from any lack of readiness or efficiency on the part of the bluejackets.[9]

The contingents from Victoria and New South Wales did not do much fighting either, but looted and burnt villages as they marched across the country.[10]

No one reading the Australian papers during the first weeks of January could avoid news about war. It overshadowed every other public matter. There were regular telegraphic reports from London about the contingents in South Africa and who had been killed in action or had died, as many of them did, from disease. Longer dispatches from correspondents provided detailed accounts, three or four weeks old, of encounters between Australian troops and the Boer forces. The correspondents avidly reported any praise of the contingents, no matter how passing or punctilious. During those few weeks at the beginning of January, new contingents departed for South Africa and others returned. Whichever way they went, large crowds welcomed or farewelled their heroes. In the cities there were enough veterans to participate in the large marches and processions. The *Sydney Morning Herald* correspondent stationed in George Street for the great procession on 1 January reported that:

> At the sight of the returned soldiers from South Africa, many still bearing traces of exposure to all weathers and the ardent rays of a veldt sun, the people raised prolonged cheers, in which there was an unmistakable ring of admiration and affection.[11]

In Perth the returned soldiers were 'undoubtedly the heroes of the day … They presented a really fine appearance, their grand physique and martial step receiving full recognition from the crowd'.[12] In Brisbane the returned soldiers attracted 'considerable attention, and drew the enthusiastic plaudits of the crowd'.[13]

When the soldiers went back to their suburbs, hometowns or rural districts they were treated as celebrities. The papers of the day have many accounts of local ceremonies. Typically, large crowds met the train or coach. As the veterans emerged they were surrounded by admiring onlookers. The mayor and aldermen, and where possible a local member of parliament, made welcoming speeches. The local rifle club or the volunteers provided guards of honour. Local brass bands played patriotic tunes. Schoolchildren, sometimes given a holiday for the occasion, joined in the procession to the local shire hall, mechanics institute, school of arts or church hall for a reception, where the ladies of the district provided tea and cakes. After formal welcomes, the veterans were typically presented with gold watches, cigar cases or other assorted mementos. Many local communities mourned the loss of young men. Committees were formed to discuss ways of raising money to commemorate the boys who didn't return.

Looking back now on the celebrations marking the foundation of the Commonwealth, it is clear that the great political and social achievements of the Australian colonies were upstaged by the glamour and excitement of a war that was far enough away to obscure the horrors of battle and the brutalisation of the Afrikaner civilian population. The community avidly grasped any praise for the performance of the troops. Pride in their putative martial abilities bulked out speeches delivered by dignitaries large and small all over the country. Addressing the celebratory procession in Rockhampton a Mr Johnson announced that the country had been

> conspicuously to the fore in the quality of courage, because we have overwhelming testimony that the Australian troops who have been fighting in South Africa are the best and the bravest. (Cheers.) So admirably have they performed the task allotted to them that their services are now more in requisition than those of any troops in the British Empire. (Applause.)[14]

In a letter to a London newspaper in the middle of January, Alfred Deakin, the attorney-general in the first federal cabinet, explained to his British readers that when the first troops departed the 'one feeling then was of anxiety that our men should acquit themselves worthily ...' But by the time of Federation 'there was no longer any doubt about their valour'. The public now watched them 'with growing exultation'. The whole continent, he declared, 'thrills with pride because of them'.[15]

But the veneration of war went beyond public applause for soldiers. It was increasingly argued that conflict itself had been a creative force in national life, welding the colonies together more effectively than decades of political debate and innumerable hours of negotiation. The editor of the influential Brisbane weekly *The Queenslander* discussed the influence of war on domestic politics. He observed that if Australians had been given the choice during the early part of 1899 of finding a way to lift Federation 'to the wave-crest of popular enthusiasm', few would have chosen war,

> but we could not have chosen any course of events better fitted to cement the Commonwealth than that which has actually marked the year. Our common experiences in this Transvaal war, our unanimous recognition of the claims of the mother-country, our universal readiness to offer treasure and life in her defence, the standing together of our soldiers in the field of battle, the singling out of Australian troops for united praise and special service, the home-coming of the invalided to all our ports – these things have given us a sense of oneness which alone would have forced federation to the front, and which now crowns the Commonwealth with a special singleness of heart.[16]

The new Australian government inherited the war from the six colonies. It had little choice in the matter. Not that there was much opposition to the ongoing engagement. There was less criticism in the new parliament than there had been in several of the colonial legislatures, but there was more to the inheritance than was immediately apparent. The tradition of involvement in imperial wars overseas had, with great speed, become deeply entrenched. None of the six colonial governments had suffered any political pain from military adventurism. Quite the reverse. The war was popular. Alfred Deakin reported that the 'martial spirit' was strong in all the colonies.[17] He explained that recruits flocked to sign up for service. After the premiers' meeting in Sydney agreed to send a further detachment to the war, four or five times the required number immediately volunteered. Opposition was limited, and diminished as the war progressed. The possibility of future military engagements grew, a development assiduously encouraged by the imperial government. The New South Wales premier, William Lyne, moved a toast to the governor-general at a state banquet on the night of 1 January and referred to the presence of the imperial troops, saying the people of Sydney had been impressed to see their soldiers marching side by side with the imperial regiments. Colonel Wyndham, the officer commanding the imperial troops at the festivities in Sydney, addressed the banquet and declared that

> in the next campaign Australia will claim it as a right to fight side by side with their English comrades ...

> we hope to see a corps, perhaps a regiment, a brigade or even an army corps, commanded by their own general and their own officers ... That is the message we have come half across the world to deliver. (Renewed cheers.)[18]

The Bulletin headed its report on the state banquet with an unexpected warning: 'The menace of militarism'. It noted that toasts were drunk for the Queen, the Prince of Wales and the royal family, the governor-general, the British Navy, the lieutenant-governors, the army and the volunteers, and only then was there a toast for the Commonwealth. Noting the numerous contemporary references to Australia's engagement in future British wars, the writer asked:

> Is this country to be a land of peace or a land of war? Are we to be a self-centred community, developing industry, promoting prosperity? ... Or are we to be a military dependency of Britain, with the flower of our youth trailed at Britain's skirts round the world wherever there is a British war? That is the question which the sending of Australians to Africa has emboldened the British to ask. Are we to have an Australian army, fed from the life blood of Australian industry, kept at the beck and call of Britain? Why should we spend blood and treasure in Britain's foreign wars? We have a task for a hundred years to come in developing our country, and establishing the happiness of our children and our children's children. Let us

> adopt the watchword once and for all: Australia for Australians and Australians for Australia.[19]

Clearly the sudden and unheralded apotheosis of the soldier worried some Australians, and particularly those who opposed the war itself. The most prominent anti-war advocate was the Victorian politician Henry Bournes Higgins, who spoke out against Australian engagement in both the colonial and federal parliaments. But his advocacy went beyond the circumstances of the war itself and examined the wider consequences of the nascent militarism. In an article published exactly one year after the founding of the Commonwealth, he posed the question of whether 'militarism and titular distinction' had pervaded Australian ideals. He recalled that some of the finest of the nation's youth had been persuaded by the lure of loyalty to 'seek distinction in the battlefields of a distant country'. The local newspapers and many public men had 'seriously put before us as a worthy aim' that young Australians should fight side by side with the regular army of the mother country 'whatever might be the cause of the war'. What do we gain, what do our children gain, he asked,

> by military parade, or by mixing in the world's quarrels, from which the remoteness of our island continent happily exempts us? We, in Australia, have no participation in the acts, no voice in the negotiations which preceded war. Our true ideal is peace – peace and internal development.

Beyond the most immediate question of involvement in overseas wars, Higgins worried about Australia itself and the likely impact of militarism on the habits and customs of the young democracy. He understood that armies were not democratic institutions and that their characteristic traditions of hierarchy and authority were antithetical to the best features of Australian life. He explained to his readers:

> There has been lately evident an effort to make use of the excitement of the South African War to drag Australia under the control of the military martinet. There is, to weak minds, something attractive – meretriciously attractive – in the gay uniforms, the plumes, the sashes, the clanking swords, the gleaming rifles, the martial stiffness of regular troops. Yet this whole system of padding, and pipe-clay, and plumage, the parade stalking of soldiers, is intensely vulgar, is absurdly untrue. Australia must make her choice between the two ideals – the ideal of militarism and the ideal of equality.[20]

The coincidence of Federation and the Boer War threw open the whole question of the relationship between Australia and the empire. It was not a new quandary. The colonial governments had all at various times had to deal with competing local and imperial interests. The emergence of Australian nationalism (see chapter 4) in the late decades of the 19th century tipped the balance one way, while the coeval movement for imperial federation (see chapter 5) pushed it in the opposite direction. Nationalist sentiment had to contend with the resurgence of European imperialism after 1870. The cross-currents persisted. The Australian colonies spent the 1890s moving towards Federation and brought the movement to fruition with a distinctive home-grown constitution. But before it could be implemented, the six colonies went to war for the empire. National pride in the active service of the colonial soldiers became hopelessly entangled with loyalty to the Queen and the empire. Federation, which was a movement for national fulfilment, came to be seen in the middle of the war as a precursor of imperial federation.

This was a favourite theme of English governors and churchmen. In an address delivered in Adelaide on 1 January, the governor of South Australia, Lord Tennyson, said that 'Imperial federation was no longer mere vision; it was an actual reality. The empire had federated on the battlefield, and the charter of federation had been sealed by the blood of many heroes'.[21] The same theme was taken up by assorted speakers during the celebrations for Australian Federation. But perhaps the most definitive statement was delivered in the official message from the secretary of state for the colonies, Joseph Chamberlain, which was read at the official ceremonies on 1 January:

> They [the British government] recognise in the long-desired consummation of the hopes of patriotic Australians a further step in the direction of the permanent unity of the British Empire, and they are satisfied that the wider powers and responsibilities

> henceforth secured to Australia will give fresh opportunity for the display of that generous loyalty and devotion to the Throne and Empire which has characterised the action in the past of its several States.[22]

The incessant rhetoric about empire created uncertainty in many minds about the character of the nation itself. One of the most popular expressions of the time was that Federation had given birth to a nation for a continent and a continent for a nation, implying that the nation was determined by geography, that it was bound by the seas that surrounded the land mass. Patriotism, the implication seemed to be, was determined by place. But there were competing views. Loyalty to Queen and empire knew no such boundaries. The empire's business was Australia's business. The interests of the empire were both ubiquitous and indivisible. If the empire was under threat in the far interior of South Africa, Australians were as personally concerned as if the enemy were threatening their own continent.

If Australian national responsibility stretched far beyond the boundaries of the continent, did local patriotism extend to include members of the 'British race' wherever they were? Did race matter more than nation? The editor of the Adelaide *Advertiser* was not alone in thinking so, declaring in an editorial on 2 January that local patriotism was 'founded on race-affinities'. Australian loyalty was not a 'proclamation of dependence or subordination, but our own sincere and spontaneous profession of unutterable loyalty and devotion to Throne and Empire'.[23] And it was so much easier to find ways to celebrate the monarchy, the empire and the military than the Constitution, the franchise or the labour movement. The symbols were ready to hand, the appropriate ceremonies known and rehearsed, the rhetoric time-tested. And behind it all towered the empire, the leaders of which had every reason to encourage colonial militarism and lavish praise on the soldiers of communities particularly susceptible to offshore flattery. The British political elite found little to admire in Australian democracy, working-class political power or egalitarian manners. The wild colonial boys were much more acceptable when uniformed, officered and at least partially disciplined.

And so a strange thing happened to Australia during 1900. At the end of the year, the long campaign for Federation came to a triumphant conclusion. An innovative and distinctive Constitution had been approved by the electorate in a series of referendums. But during the first week of the new century it was not Australia's great political and social achievements that received the attention but the imperial war of conquest in South Africa. Almost overnight, soldiers came to be seen as embodying the national spirit. War eclipsed constitution-making. Imperial loyalty overwhelmed Australian nationalism. The largest question has rarely been asked. There is no doubt these developments were welcomed in London, but to what extent was this outcome consciously planned by the imperial government?

It was symptomatic of the Australian situation in January 1901 that there were none of those occasions, ubiquitous during independence ceremonies all over the world, that saw a lowering of an old imperial flag and the raising of a new national one. There was no national flag in 1901. There were colonial flags, but the Union Jack continued to be flown throughout Australia until the middle of the 20th century, and protocol demanded that it must be flown in a higher position than any other flag. The initiative for creating new flags came from the imperial government, Chamberlain writing to the governor-general in November 1900 indicating the need for a Commonwealth flag. But it was mandatory to devise a flag that would do no more than create a distinctive design to add to the Union Jack, or to 'deface the fly' as the formal language of flags described it. So the competition conducted during 1901, which attracted 30 000 entries, was to find designs to embellish the British red and blue ensigns. It was not to create a distinctive national flag. And even then the designs had to be sent to Britain for approval, which took almost a year to receive. The official designs of the two flags, the red and blue ensigns, were not published in the *Commonwealth Gazette* until February 1903. The blue ensign only became the official national flag with the passage of the Flag Act of 1953, the preamble of which recognised that the Australian flag was the British blue ensign.

The radicals at the Sydney *Bulletin* were scornful. The flag was vulgar, ill-fitting, with no artistic virtue, no national significance. Minds move slowly and the nation was 'still Britain's little boy':

> What more natural than that he should accept his father's cut-down garments? … That bastard flag is a true symbol of the bastard state of Australian opinion, still in large part biased by British traditions, British customs, still lacking many years to the sufficiency of manhood, which will determine the path of its own.[24]

But the relationship between colonies and imperial authorities, the question as to sovereignty and the matter of defence against possible enemies – these questions had already hung above colonial life during the second half of the 19th century, as they had done in empires across time.

3

Colonial defence: Australia or empire?

The Boer War, we have already argued, was as much of a watershed for the Australian colonies as Federation. Both represented a definitive answer to questions that had been debated but remained unresolved during the second half of the 19th century, particularly when Britain was at war in the Crimea in the 1850s and in Africa in the 1880s. How independent were the five colonies that had their own parliaments? Did they have any capacity to develop relations with foreign powers? Were they automatically involved in Britain's assorted wars or was neutrality a possible option? Was there an obligation to provide assistance to the mother country? If so, was it legal or merely moral? How responsible were the colonies for their own defence? The leading British historian Edward Freeman appreciated that these questions were of critical importance. War, he saw, was the inescapable test of the constitutional and legal standing of the colonies and their place in the world. Writing in 1886, he observed:

> the fullest independence in local affairs cannot wholly put out of sight the fact that in all strictly national affairs the freest of colonies is as dependent as ever. The greatest and freest of colonies may at any moment find itself plunged into a war which may suit the interests or the fancies of the people of Great Britain, but which may in no way suit the interests or the fancies of the people of the colony.[1]

Federation did not change the situation. The new Commonwealth had no greater autonomy than the individual colonies had been able to exercise after 1856. It remained shackled to the Colonial Office.

The outbreak of the Crimean War in 1854 had inspired one of the first public debates about colonial responsibilities at a time of international conflict. In May, prominent Sydney citizens called a public meeting for the purpose of 'expressing their continued loyalty and attachment to Her Majesty'. Sir Charles Nicholson, speaker of the Legislative Council, declared that the impending war was one 'which would enlist the sympathies of every right-thinking patriotic man'. He also spoke of the colonist's determination 'to maintain to the utmost of their ability to honour the British flag, and the security of this portion of Her Majesty's

Empire'. Nicholson's fellow councillor JB Darvall, directly addressing the audience, announced that 'your country' is on the verge of war. 'That is enough to stir the blood of every Briton – England is at war! … It becomes you', he thundered, 'to assert your readiness at all events to perform whatever duty may be cast upon you in the impending struggle'. He was assured that there was but one feeling abroad – 'that of allegiance and loyalty to your Sovereign. There never was a time when a more welcome echo of the enthusiasm and loyalty so ardently felt in England, would be heard from New South Wales'. The patriotic speeches were constantly applauded.[2]

But the spirit of unquestioned support for Britain was abruptly challenged when the prominent Presbyterian cleric John Dunmore Lang mounted the stage. He began by objecting to the people of New South Wales 'isolated, as they were … pronouncing an opinion on a war in Europe'. The newspaper reporter noted in response to this there was 'great confusion, in which groans and cheers were mingled'. Lang said he did not ask whether the war was just or not because in either case the colony 'had nothing to do with it'. Once again hisses competed with cheers. The colonists, he insisted, were not 'called upon to interfere in European wars'. What had they to do with it? By throwing their weight behind Britain the colonists ran the risk of bringing the war into the Pacific. The promoters of the meeting, he argued, were contemplating action of great seriousness which would potentially 'transfer the Pacific Ocean, never before the seat of war, into a battle-field for the nations of Europe'.

Lang returned to the question four years later when rumours were widespread about a possible war between Britain and France. In a public lecture he began by reminding his audience of George Washington's valedictory injunction that the United States remain clear of all entangling European alliances and the successful result of that policy. He went on to point out the dangers that would arise if New South Wales became involved in the conflict, and the cost of providing for home defence. His solution to the problem was radically simple. He had prepared a draft petition requesting the British government at once 'to concede to us, with all necessary guarantees and stipulations our entire freedom and national independence, and to recognise these Australian colonies from thenceforth as sovereign and Independent States'.

With such a status the colonies could take advantage of their isolated location and remain detached from the wars of Europe while maintaining friendly relations with all the great powers. Central to Lang's argument was that the legal and constitutional ties with Britain were not an advantage but a certain source of danger that would lead the colonies into unwanted wars. The urgent necessity for the 'progressive and rapid settlement of these colonies', for the development of their various and vast resources, demanded that their inhabitants 'should enjoy uninterrupted peace with all mankind'. The argument was further developed in the fourth clause of the petition, which read:

> That situated, moreover, as these colonies are, at a vast distance from all other parts of the civilised world,

> and entirely isolated as they are both from Europe and America, there can be no reasonable ground for apprehension of their ever coming into hostile collision, as self-governing political communities with any other portion of the human race.[3]

A year later Lang took his cause into the fledgling New South Wales parliament in response to a debate about the future defence of the colony, arguing that there was much reason to fear that Britain would sooner or later be involved in war with one or more of the great European powers. In a notice of motion he declared:

> That in such an event, the whole of the Australian Colonies … although isolated from the rest of mankind by surrounding oceans, and having no conceivable interest or concern in any European contest, will, nevertheless, as part and parcel of the British Empire, be immediately involved in all the hardships and calamities of war …

His reiterated solution was the creation of a 'Sovereign and Independent Australian Empire'.[4]

Lang was endlessly controversial and combative. Newspaper reports of meetings he addressed suggested that while he was usually in a minority he had a small following. But his importance for us is that he raised questions that continued to have relevance for generations. This was particularly so when he outlined his distinctive variety of colonial patriotism. Charged by outraged opponents with disloyalty and even with treason, he explained that he saw patriotism as the duty to seek the good of the land 'in which we dwell'. And it was here that he drew together his attitude to Britain and his prescription for local defence: 'Will any man tell me', he asked, 'that it is seeking the good of these Australian colonies to involve a million of people *here* at the ends of the earth in all the calamities of war?' And the war would be with a people and nations on the other side of the globe 'with whom, as Australian Colonists, we have never had any quarrel'.[5] He hammered the message home in speeches and letters to the press. Writing to the Melbourne *Argus* in 1858 he asked:

> But will any man tell me that it can ever be the duty of an Australian patriot to seek to involve his adopted country, with its million of inhabitants, in the calamities of war whenever, in the complicated maze of European politics, Great Britain chooses to go to war with France, or any other great Power, as we know she has done too often, and without the slightest necessity, already?[6]

Lang's ideas were taken up by others in the 1870s and 1880s, when they assumed greater significance as the colonists were forced to deal with two powerful, competing movements: a burgeoning local patriotism and imperial federation. The Victorian parliament debated the relations between colony and empire over three nights in December 1869 in response to the establishment by expatriate, imperial-minded colonists in London of what became the Royal Colonial Institute. Familiar themes ran through the debate. Would the colonies become independent and follow the path taken by the United States? Was the imperial government encouraging the colonies of settlement to take that course? James McCulloch argued that there was

> no doubt that separation will come some day. This colony will some day be disunited from England. Probably certain people will think that this language partakes somewhat of treason, but as sure as the United States separated from England, so sure will this colony of Victoria be, sometime, separated also.[7]

GV Smith noted that while his contemporaries were affected by the sentimental ties that bound them to England, 'we must remember that our children will not be so affected'.[8]

As was the case in debates about relations with Britain, the question of defence was always present. The prominent liberal George Higinbotham was confident that Victoria could defend itself. Given its situation in 'a remote corner of the world … no land force could attack' the colony 'in such power as to be able to resist the weakest of our colonial defences upon land'.[9] But his colleague from Gippsland, Dr GD Macartney, provided a more sobering assessment of the potential danger to the colony as a result of the connection with Britain. There were, he judged, some benefits in imperial membership, but he wanted to know at what price, observing that:

> We have a British connexion now – we are united to one of the greatest nations on earth. There is pride in that; but, after all, it is sentimentality. Let us take the real state of things, and look it in the face. At what price do we possess this British connexion? It is at the expense of the risk of devastation, plunder, and bloodshed, in time of war. Looking at the question in a practical point of view, this must be the opinion of every honorable member. Are the benefits which we enjoy, as part of the British Empire, such as to compensate us for running this risk?

Victoria itself had no enemies and was not under any threat, Macartney arguing that:

> There is not a single country from which Victoria has at the present time any reason to anticipate war. Whence then has war to come? Whence is invasion to come? Only when England becomes involved in a war with one of the great nations of the world. A state of relationship ought to be brought about between Victoria and the mother country which would save this colony from the consequences of such a calamity ...[10]

Within a few months of this debate the relationship with Britain became a more immediate concern. The imperial government decided to recall the last of its troops from Australia and New Zealand. Old colonists lamented. The classically trained recalled the withdrawal of the Roman legions from Britain. In Victoria, a royal commission was established to consider the necessity of a federal union of the Australian colonies. The advantages of Federation were powerfully made:

> It enlarges the home market, which is the nursing mother of native manufactures. It forms larger designs, engages in larger enterprises, and by its increased resources and authority causes them to be more speedily accomplished. It obtains additional security for peace by increasing its means of defence; and, by creating a nation, it creates along with it the sentiment of nationality ...[11]

The royal commission took a far more controversial turn when, in the third section of its first report, it addressed the question of the neutrality of the colonies in war, pointing to the circumstances created by the withdrawal of British troops:

> The British Colonies from which the Imperial troops have been wholly withdrawn present the unprecedented phenomenon of responsibility without either corresponding authority or adequate protection. They are as liable to all the hazards of war as the United Kingdom; but they can influence the commencement or continuance of war no more than they can control the movements of the solar system; and they have no certain assurance of that aid against an enemy upon which integral portions of the United

> Kingdom can confidently reckon. This is a relation so wanting in mutuality that it cannot safely be regarded as a lasting one ...[12]

The proposed solution was to seek from Britain the power to enter into treaties and agreements with foreign powers and assume the responsibilities of a sovereign state, including the capacity to remain neutral in the event of war involving the imperial government.

The eleven-man commission was divided over the question of neutrality, although only two members came out against the idea. The press in Melbourne was equally divided. The *Age* argued that when colonies defended themselves they must be allowed

> independent volition as to when it shall begin or leave off fighting ... The concession of a neutral flag to the colonies would relieve them from the grievous wrong of being forced into a war by statesmen who owe them no responsibility.[13]

The *Argus* doubted the possibility of achieving neutrality without totally unacceptable institutional changes, observing that:

> We may execute a national declaration of alienage, and renounce our allegiance to the Queen. We shall then certainly become neutrals, if we choose to pay the necessary price for neutrality. Or we may make up our minds loyally to follow, for better or for worse, the

> fortunes of England in peace and in war. We have little doubt what the choice of this colony will be.[14]

Similar views were expressed by the major intercolonial newspapers. The *Sydney Morning Herald* recognised that the great difficulty faced by the colonies was 'the danger of being involved in the risks of war – one which must be always great, and against which no adequate security has been yet devised'.[15]

But fifteen years later New South Wales became involved in an imperial campaign in a manner not envisaged by anyone who debated the question in 1870. War did not encroach on a peaceful community minding its business. The government in Sydney made a sudden decision early in 1885 to send a contingent of 700 troops to assist a British campaign in the Sudan following the death in Khartoum of the charismatic General Charles Gordon. The troops were sent, without the prior approval of parliament, by the attorney-general and acting premier, WB Dalley. By the time parliament met, the contingent was halfway to Africa. A debate that stretched over five nights ended with a strong endorsement of the government's precipitate action while providing a valuable compendium of contemporary parliamentary opinion about war and peace, the colonies and the empire. By a two-thirds majority the Legislative Assembly passed the following motion:

> We desire to express our hearty approval of the conduct of the ministers in despatching the Australian contingent to aid the imperial forces in Egypt; and

> we regard their action as manifesting the loyalty of the Australian people to the Crown, and as drawing more closely together the various portions of our great empire.[16]

On the passage of the motion members rose and gave three cheers for the Queen.

During the debate they made constant reference to their 'loyalty' even when criticising the government. But the idea of loyalty was of central importance. It clearly stood in the way of more searching debate then and later. And while British ministers were one thing, the monarch was a different matter. The Queen's sanction of British foreign policy put it beyond criticism by members who expressed their 'deep and unfeigned attachment to her most gracious Majesty's throne and person'.[17]

But supporters of the contingent provided many reasons why they were willing to overlook and excuse the clear illegality of the government's action. The most uncomplicated justification from numerous members was simply declaring that they were Englishmen and were automatically involved in imperial adventures. John See from Grafton explained that 'our pulses beat in unison with those of the people of England, notwithstanding that we are separated by so many thousands of miles of ocean'.[18] Robert Wisdom confessed that he hoped he would always be able to boast that he was an Englishman, which 'was the proudest boast any man can make; I mean a subject of the empire, not of any particular part'.[19] The veteran politician Sir John Robertson said that when he heard colonists say the members of the contingent were not British soldiers his reply was: 'I believe the heart of a Briton is in every one of them'.[20] His colleague Arthur Ryrie asked rhetorically: 'Are not Queen Victoria's enemies the enemies of New South Wales wherever and whoever they may be?'[21] Any blow to imperial prestige touched the colonists as well. 'Let England be humiliated', JP Abbott, declared, no matter when or how, 'these colonies are bound to share in that humiliation'.[22]

Members showed little desire to examine the nature of the conflict in the Sudan or consider matters of law or morality. Louis Heydon argued that all such arguments were 'utterly beside the question' because it was 'not open to us here to weigh the question of the justice or otherwise of the war'.[23] Sir John Robertson observed:

> Be it right or be it wrong for England to be in Egypt, I hold that if we expect England to stand by us in any trouble we ought to stand by England in her troubles, and rely on the Parliament and people of the mother country to see that no injustice is done to any people by her forces.[24]

While imperial sentiment was uppermost in the rhetoric, there was calculation as well. EA Baker confided in his colleagues that when in the future the Australian colonies were in danger from a foreign foe, the English would never forget 'the handsome way in which New South Wales offered this small assistance to them in their time of danger'.[25] There was excitement too in military adventure. Old Sir John Robertson confessed that never in his life did his blood 'so thrill with emotion' as when he saw the men and horses march down to Circular Quay.[26] He was not alone in his excitement. GC Loughnan found that as the troops departed his 'English blood' pulsed through his veins 'more hotly than it did at any time in my youth'.[27]

For many of the members of the parliament, the dispatch of the contingent had transformed the colony. 'We have fairly begun our military career', declared the member for Orange, William Clarke, and many members agreed.[28] LF Heydon thought that his colleagues had made history. In fact, with the departure of the troops, 'our history may be truly said to begin'. Up to the present time the legislature had been 'little more than a municipal body' but now 'this country has risen to the stature of nationhood, and we are a nation's parliament henceforth'.[29] This was a common view. RC Luscombe believed the adventure would raise 'the Australian colonies in the estimation of the nations of the earth'.[30] In the Legislative Council, Sir Alfred Stephen added his authority to the proposition that people in all the colonies regarded the dispatch of the contingent as an event calculated to raise the character of the community 'more than all that could have been effected for us by any … other efforts of our own'.[31]

Parliamentary colleagues in the other colonies agreed with these sentiments. In the Victorian parliament, David Gaunson said that he believed the troops had 'made the name of Australia respected throughout the world'. He explained that they were 'formerly so little thought of that they were not fond of admitting themselves to be Australians'. But public opinion had 'so changed that a man can say with pride that he is from Australia'.[32] Angus Mackay thought the venture was, 'the greatest historical event in the history of Australia'.[33] For others, the 'honour and glory' of the expedition had 'erected Australia into a nation'.[34] This was a view endorsed by CH Pearson, the most intellectually distinguished member of all the colonial parliaments. He had been in Britain when the decision to intervene had been made. It had, he declared 'sent a thrill through the whole English-speaking world'. He explained:

> I can answer for it that the effect produced by that offer in England was one to which it would seem there has scarcely been anything comparable … But a community that shows itself able to rise to the level of great decision, and prepared to throw in its fortunes with the mother country, and associate itself with the perils and toils of empire, is one that must be admitted into the family of nations, and become thenceforward a power among them, its sons being respected wherever they go.[35]

Despite such enthusiastic endorsement, the Sudan venture attracted criticism both within the parliaments and among the electorate. The flouting of parliamentary practice continued to agitate sections of the community, but other critics reached beyond the constitutional question to consider the broader matter of the appropriate relations between the Australian colonies and the imperial government. At the heart of the debate was the inescapable question of war. While many supporters of the New South Wales government were caught up in the glamour and excitement of the Sudan adventure, sceptics questioned the legitimacy of the whole campaign. In the Victorian parliament, James Mirams, the member for Collingwood, was emphatic is his criticism, announcing: 'I say unhesitatingly that this country did wrong, absolutely wrong, when it offered to send a contingent to engage in such a miserable, such a mean, such a contemptible, and such an unholy fight …'[36]

Critics who questioned the need for the involvement were strengthened in their convictions when the contingent returned without any combat experience. But on both sides of the debate, activists believed that an important precedent had been set. The imperialists looked forward to future military involvement. Sudan was a demonstration of Australia's 'right to take our part in the empire's struggles, and … proof of our willingness to fight and bleed for the empire'.[37] The opposition dreaded that prospect, believing that the colonies were courting avoidable conflict. In the New South Wales parliament, Angus Cameron regretted the fact that the government had foolishly thrust itself forward into conflict when the colony's 'geographical position almost gave us immunity from an attack by an enemy …'[38] His colleague MJ Hammond feared the Sudan adventure would 'involve the country ever after in European complications that we should be much better free from'. He maintained that

> while we have at this early stage of our history every right to prepare to defend ourselves, we have no right to wantonly mix up with the hereditary troubles of

> England … What can this colony gain, or what good can we do, by mixing up with them uncalled for?[39]

AJ Gould was equally concerned with the precedent that had been established. We have, he said,

> to look at the future liability, at the great departure we have taken, and also to remember that we have laid down the principle that we are now prepared to enter into England's wars, and to assist her with troops. Having done it now we shall be expected to do it again in the future.[40]

They were concerns echoed by the member for Newcastle, James Fletcher, who remarked:

> Hitherto we have lived at peace with the whole world … We have been supposed to be weak, but in my opinion our very weakness has been our great strength. We have been neutral, and our neutrality has been our safeguard. What have we done now? We have published to the world that New South Wales is prepared to assist in fighting the battles of England, whether England is in the right or in the wrong.

Fletcher was not a pacifist, rather a colonial patriot suggesting that the local community

> publish to the world the fact that while living in peace with the nations of the earth … we value this territory

> of New South Wales so dearly that if any one were to attempt to take one inch of it they would have to take it over the dead bodies of every man in the country.[41]

The most radical challenge to the imperialists came from the member for Mudgee, David Buchanan. He ridiculed what they proudly called their 'duty' and their 'loyalty'. The duty of the colonists was to 'stand upon this ground, and never either now or hereafter send a soldier from our shores'; it was to 'defend ourselves against attack by repelling invaders, and we have no duty cast upon us to do anything else'. And the war in the Sudan was a disreputable one, fought against people who were struggling for their freedom. The Australians had gone to fight against men who had never done harm to them 'and who have never seen them in the face'. The fundamental problem was the continuing connection with Britain. Separation would render Australia 'safer, more secure, and happier in every sense of the word'. Without independence, Australia was in constant danger from Britain. 'It stands to reason', he thundered, 'that separation is the true policy of this country'. Responding to a chorus of 'no, no', he declared:

> The reason why I say that the true policy of this country is to separate from England, is that England in the midst of European complications is always liable to be immersed in war with some of the great European states, and the misery to us is that from our political connection – which has yielded us nothing – every enemy of England becomes an enemy of ours; that the

> same enemy which is fighting England may strike a blow at us. Why should we incur that danger?[42]

The New South Wales contingent had a brief and unspectacular sojourn in the war zone. The troops had no direct combat experience and after less than seven weeks set sail for home. Several men died of typhoid before the expedition returned and a few more succumbed on the return journey. It was hard to replicate the wild public enthusiasm of the departure a few months before. A period in quarantine was followed by a march up from the Quay in drenching rain, but official Australia provided a chorus of support and admiration. Representatives from the other colonies delivered patriotic speeches and were unanimous in their assessment of the epochal significance of the intervention. Sir George Verdon, representing Victoria, wished New South Wales 'joy of one of the grandest and most significant events in the history of Australia'. 'You have', he declared, 'crossed the Rubicon which separates a prosperous, rich, and peaceful community from a nation, animated by the feelings of honour, chivalry, and a sense of public duty ...'[43] The Queen and the imperial commander-in-chief sent telegrams. Imperial patronage rewarded the participants in proportion to their status. The soldiers received campaign medals, the senior officers awards of one sort or another, and WB Dalley became the first Australian elevated to the Privy Council.

Threaded through the abundant rhetoric was the belief that the dispatch of the contingent had international significance. The Queensland representative Lieutenant

Colonel Mein thought that the affair had demonstrated to the world that Australian patriotism was not restricted to the land that gave it birth but 'embraces the whole Empire of Britain'. It was a view shared by the New South Wales governor, Lord Augustus Loftus, who asserted that 'for purposes of defence there has been practically now established an Imperial federation'.[44]

It was a prospect that cheered the British military officers and governors serving in Australia, and implied the possibility of future expeditionary forces. This hope grew among the political elite in Britain, and in their assessment of British military strength they increasingly came to count the putative contribution of troops from Australia, Canada, New Zealand and South Africa. In a speech on relations with the United States and the colonies delivered in 1888, the leading British politician Joseph Chamberlain considered whether the settler colonies would necessarily follow the American road to separation. He believed that sentiment and loyalty would keep them in their place and avoid republican independence. 'I have heard it argued', he said,

> that the colonies would be very foolish to allow themselves to become mixed up in our old-world policy, and to concern themselves with wars in which they can have no possible interest or advantage. But I may point to the action of the colonies not so very long ago in the case of the Egyptian war – (hear, hear) – when they exhibited a sentiment … on an occasion in which they certainly had nothing but a sentimental interest.[45]

Chamberlain's lecture indicates that in the 1880s, British leaders still worried that the settler colonies would follow the example of the United States. They worked strenuously, and as it turned out successfully, to see that it did not happen. But their concern was an indication that a distinctive Australian patriotism was a force to be reckoned with, threatening what the British called separatism at a time when they increasingly felt the need to keep the large settler colonies locked into dependency. We should now turn our attention to colonial patriotism.

4

Australia's radical patriots

When the First Fleet arrived in Australia in January 1788, the new American republic was five years old. The thirteen colonies had defeated the British army and had declared their independence. Some of the officers and soldiers arriving in Sydney Cove had served in that war. The global struggle between empire and nation that received its original impetus from the successful American rebellion has, therefore, accompanied Australian history from the very beginning. So too have the competing attractions of imperial, aristocratic Britain and republican, democratic America. Australians with an interest in the wider world have, across many generations, witnessed a continuing sequence of nationalist rebellion against the great empires.

During the first generation of settlement in New South Wales and Van Diemen's Land, the Americas were transformed. Between 1810 and 1830 the whole of Central and South America rebelled against the Spanish, Portuguese and French empires. Sixteen new independent republics were created and joined the concert of nations. The European provinces of the Ottoman empire rebelled, and the great powers threw their weight behind Greek independence, which was formally achieved in 1832. By then nationalists were agitating for independence in all parts of Europe from the Ottoman, Tsarist, Hapsburg and British empires. Nationalism inspired artists, writers and musicians in every part of Europe where distinctive peoples were striving to break free from the grip of empire and establish sovereign states. Every national movement had its idealists and theorists, but the most influential prophet of the nation-state was the Italian activist-philosopher Giuseppe Mazzini, who believed:

> Humanity will not be truly constituted until all the peoples that form it, having won the free exercise of their sovereignty, are united in a republican federation. Nationhood is sacred. The Pact of Humanity cannot be signed by individuals, but by free and equal peoples with a name, a flag and a consciousness of their own life ... God has prescribed the affirmation of its nationhood to every people as the part it must play in the work of humanity: this is the mission, the task that each people must perform upon earth in order that the Divine Idea may be realized in the world.[1]

Empires went out of fashion in Britain itself in the early 19th century. Intellectual leaders as prominent as Adam Smith and Jeremy Bentham questioned the value of colonies, and the development of relations with the independent United States bore out their scepticism. Economic links with the republic grew stronger after the War of Independence. Trade burgeoned, and neither American sovereignty nor republican institutions hampered large-scale British investment or massive Anglo-Irish immigration. Britain's adoption of free trade placed the colonies in the same position as foreign states and undermined established arguments about the economic benefits of colonies.

The leaders of the free trade cause, such as Richard Cobden and John Bright, were sceptical about the whole imperial project. They thought of it as associated with the domestic aristocracy and as the source of endless wars and needless foreign intervention. 'The vulgar kind of patriotic sentiment', Cobden wrote, 'leads its professors to exult in military interventions'.[2] Bright was a vehement critic of imperial wars, often equating killing in pursuit of national objectives with murder. British prosperity, the free traders believed, was dependent on commerce, industry and trade with the whole world, which required peace and was disrupted by war. Free trade was good for business but it was much more than that. Indeed it was, in Cobden's view, the only means of effecting 'universal and permanent peace'.[3] And free trade would be the solvent of empire:

> The colonial system, with all its dazzling appeals to the passions of the people, can never be got rid of

> except by the indirect process of Free Trade, which will gradually and imperceptibly loose the bands which unite our Colonies to us by a mistaken notion of self-interest.[4]

Cobden took a close interest in Canada, which he believed should become independent, arguing in 1865 that

> We are two peoples to all intents and purposes, and it is a perilous delusion to both parties to attempt to keep up a sham connexion and dependence which will snap asunder if it ever should be put to the strain of stern reality ... In my opinion it is for the interest of both that we should as speedily as possible sever the political thread by which we are as communities connected, and leave the individuals on both sides to cultivate the relations of commerce and friendly intercourse as with other nations.[5]

Following the great era of rebellion in the Americas, it became a common and understandable assumption that colonies would naturally pass from childhood to maturity, at which point they would seek to gain their independence as sovereign nation-states. But the situation of Britain's self-governing colonies was distinctive in many ways. They had their own parliamentary institutions from the middle of the 19th century but they were still dependent societies without external sovereignty and, despite their size, population and robust economies, not nation-states like the South and Central American republics. Nor was their situation comparable with the so-called captive nations ruled by foreign overlords and repressed by their armies. They had a wide range of freedoms but these did not extend beyond their borders. They had no standing on the world stage.

The specific problems associated with the relations between the settler colonies and imperial Britain received their most searching examination in the many works of Goldwin Smith, a leading English academic who migrated first to the United States and then to Canada. In a series of articles and books published between 1860 and the early years of the 20th century, he sought to define the appropriate relations between Canada, Britain and the United States. His work was peculiarly relevant to Australia, and was widely read locally, judging by the frequent references to it during debates in the colonial parliaments. His first essays on the empire were published in a London newspaper in 1861 and, with the strong support of Richard Cobden, appeared in book form two years later.[6] Nations, he argued,

> like men, are intended by nature to form their own character by self-exertion and self-control. They have in them the faculties of political life, which they must develop, as we did, by their own efforts. Every hour that an adult Colony is kept in leading strings, a mischief is done to its political character from which it may hereafter recover no doubt, but at the expense of great suffering and disaster … They have a right above all … to be released from the childish thraldom which,

> if it is prolonged, will be fatal to their hope of attaining the manly strength and stature of great nations.[7]

Having lived in both Canada and the United States, Smith was able to make trenchant comparisons between the two, as he did in one of his best-known books, *The Political Destiny of Canada*, published in 1877. On almost every count Canada did not measure up to the neighbouring republic, due in very large measure to its dependent colonial status, which stunted the development of indigenous institutions and national self-realisation. Dependence on Britain had far-reaching consequences, but above all it was unnatural. 'One tree', he declared, 'might as well be set to regulate the growth of another tree, as one nation to regulate the growth of another nation' and, in the case in question, the two trees were 'of different sorts and planted under different skies'.[8]

Without independence there was no sense of nationality and no patriotism. In a dependency there was no love of or pride in country. Every bond, every interest was stronger than country. In place of national pride there was a 'restless and self-abasing effort to attract the notice of the superior country'.[9] Want of nationality was 'attended, too, with a certain want of self-respect, not only political but social … Wealthy men in a dependency are inclined to look to the imperial country as the social centre and the goal of their social ambition, if not their ultimate abode …'[10]

A continuing feature of colonial dependence was the tie with the monarchy and the Crown's local servants, the provincial governors. It all ran counter to the reality of politics in the new world and could furnish no sound basis for government 'in the soil of reason and equality'. In Canada the monarchy did much evil by blinding public men and the people generally to the real requirements of the situation and hiding the reality that in a democracy power comes from the people. In fact, 'The hereditary principle was dead at its root ... and its age had passed away in the more advanced portion of humanity ...'[11] The continuing links with Britain made it less likely that the Canadian provinces would develop their own distinctive institutions, because 'constitutions are not made but grow; and ... to be strong and respected, they must be developed by a nation itself out of the elements of its own character and circumstances, not imposed on it, however benevolently, from without'.[12]

Political activists in the Australian colonies lacked Goldwin Smith's international standing, but they shared many of his ideas and objectives. JD Lang followed a similar intellectual path. In 1870, reacting to the withdrawal of British troops, he brought together much of his previous work in his book *The Coming Event! Or Freedom and Independence for the Seven United Provinces of Australia*, which was published in London. Addressing the 'electors of the city of Sydney', he declared that as a result of the British withdrawal a great question had been 'virtually submitted for our decision'. Were the Australian colonies 'to remain for an indefinite period' dependencies of Britain or assume the 'noble position of a Sovereign and Independent State'? The main object of the book was to recommend to all parties at home and abroad 'the speedy and entire political Separation of the United Colonies of Australia from the mother country, and their erection into a Sovereign and Independent State'.[13]

Lang brought together attitudes to nationalism similar to Mazzini's with perceptive observations about the emergence of what he called colonial nationality. He described the way the settler came to feel at ease in the new world as memories of the homeland 'became fainter and fainter'. The colony itself eventually 'engrosses all his affections', and the idea of the welfare and advancement of his adopted country, 'like a new passion, takes possession of his soul'. The resulting emergence of the spirit of colonial nationality was no accidental feeling. It was 'unquestionably of Divine implantation … designed not for evil but for good'. The nation itself was part of God's plan for mankind. The great diversity of the world predisposed communities to have feelings, interests and objects 'centred in their own country or territory, and differing, in that particular, from those of every other portion of the human race'. The Australian colonies, separated by vast distances from the homeland and occupying a unique physical environment, would 'infallibly become a nation'. The grouping of mankind into nations was evidently a divine ordinance, designed for the welfare and advancement of the human race. It was, therefore, both 'the law of nature' and 'the ordinance of God' that the colonies should have 'their freedom and independence'. Empires were not only politically oppressive, they defied the divine plan for mankind. Its contemporary unfolding could be seen in the 'ongoing reconstruction of oppressed nationalities' in Europe, which, Lang believed, was 'the miracle of the age'.[14]

Lang also believed that the British Empire and loyalty to it held back the unfolding of colonial patriotism, even when imperial intentions were benign. Above all, continuing attachment to the old homeland smothered the feeling of nationality, which was

> the very soul of society, which animates and exults the whole brother-hood of associated men … And must the young Australian be debarred from the exercise of that generous and manly feeling, of which every rightly constituted mind is conscious, when he exclaims, with deep emotion, 'This is my own, my native land!'[15]

Lang did bring his analysis down to earth. In particular he argued that the Australian colonies had already attained what he called their 'political majority'. They were consequently entitled to their freedom and independence. And the evidence adduced was substantial. The combined population of the colonies was already more than one and a half million and was increasing rapidly. It was already greater than the population of some of the world's smaller sovereign states. The material resources of the colonies in terms of wealth and revenue were unquestionably superior to those of any other similar-sized community. But colonial political achievements were even more significant. The facility and success with which the representative institutions had been brought into full operation was, Lang believed, surely a sufficient and satisfactory proof of the fitness of the colonies for complete self-government. He ticked off the reforms – secret ballot, manhood suffrage, selection legislation, public education, equal electoral districts. When, he asked rhetorically, 'has there ever been enacted in so short a period of time, even in England, such a series of reforms as those which this goodly catalogue presents?'[16]

Like Goldwin Smith, Lang believed that progress towards independence required a break with the monarchy and the establishment of a republic. The fact was, there was 'no other form of government either practical or possible, in a British colony obtaining its freedom and independence, than that of a republic'. Why, asked Lang, should we be either 'unwilling or afraid' to take that vital step?[17]

And then there was the ever-present question of war and aggression, and whether independent colonies could defend themselves. Lang returned to a position he had been promoting for years: Australia was so isolated there was no danger of external aggression. Geography was the most certain guarantee of Australia's security. He turned to the history of the Latin American republics and their established ability to remain detached from European conflict. He was encouraged too by the long history of United States neutrality and sought to emulate it. 'The fact is', he wrote,

> the only chance we have of hearing of war in any shape in Australia for a century to come, lies in our connection with Great Britain, as a group of her many dependencies. And considering the warlike propensities of our worthy mother … our chance of peace under her wing is at best but very precarious.[18]

Lang had first developed his hopes about the 'Coming Event' as far back as 1850, in two public lectures that were subsequently published locally. In the intervening twenty years much had changed, but the great historic event he sought was as far away as ever. The colonies had established their own parliaments and, as Lang conceded, they had carried through a substantial agenda of democratic reform. And much of Lang's program had stalled, partly because of the very success of the domestic political agenda and the imperial government's policy of conceding a large measure of political autonomy to the self-governing colonies. There was, consequently, little support for separation from Britain in the fledgling parliaments or for a republic, although, as we have seen, the withdrawal of imperial troops had led to a renewed discussion of future defence policy. Though loyalty to the monarch, political dependence and war were often treated as separate issues, they were inextricably enmeshed. Without external sovereignty or the capacity to deal directly with foreign powers, the colonies were potentially committed in advance to Britain's wars. And as the empire grew, so did the locations and occasions of potential conflict. Critics of empire, both at home and in the colonies, were aware that Britain was an aggressive, belligerent power almost continuously at war during the 19th century. There were at least fifty wars large and small during that time, more than twenty of them between 1856 and 1900. Britain was fighting somewhere in the world almost every year during the second half of the 19th century. The Pax Britannica was a blood-soaked business. Can there be any wonder that for some Australians empire meant war? They feared, with prescience, that it would eventually catch up with the colonies, their isolation notwithstanding.

Fear and anxiety about war was a common feature of colonial life. The Australian newspapers provided on-going accounts of European politics that became much more immediate after the connection of the colonies by telegraphic cables. Rumours about impending war were instantly relayed to the colonies. An article on war scares in Australia in the 19th century estimated that there were forty-five involving England's international engagements during the century.[19] The more substantial ones concerned fear of Russian attack during the Crimean War in the 1850s, and during tension over Afghanistan in 1878 and 1885. In 1859 the fear was about a French attack, the possibility of which appeared far more realistic after the annexation of New Caledonia in 1853. German colonial expansion into the Pacific in the 1880s added another potential aggressor. Colonial anxiety was understandable. There was no way for the Australians to know what might happen on the other side of the world nor any possibility of exercising even marginal influence on British policy, which was never discussed with the colonial governments. During a debate in the Victorian parliament on colonial defence in 1882, the cosmopolitan CH Pearson observed that 'for the last ten years during which repeated scares had prevailed, the state of Europe had been such that war might have broken out at any moment. No man could say when war would not break out'.[20]

In the aftermath of the Sudan adventure there was

much discussion in both Britain and Australia about further and perhaps permanent defence cooperation. Military and naval lobbyists sought ways to tie the large settler colonies into imperial defence strategy, and looked forward to a future where shared burdens would prepare the way for eventual imperial federation. More pragmatic analysts just wanted the prosperous colonies to contribute to the high cost of defending a worldwide empire. Colonial politicians sought the protection of a British naval flotilla based in and confined to Australian waters. They were willing to contribute modestly to the resulting costs. An agreement was eventually negotiated at an imperial conference in London in 1887 and taken back for ratification to the colonial parliaments, where there was much to consider. There was the question of who should be responsible for protecting the maritime trade routes where British merchant ships carried the colonies' exports and imports. Could the flotilla be deployed wherever the Admiralty desired in time of war? But even more searching, abiding questions arose. Would closer defence ties with Britain make Australia more or less vulnerable? Were the warships liabilities that provided protection against Britain's enemies with which the colonies themselves had no cause to quarrel? Was the empire itself both founded on and held together by violence? Was it more cockpit than haven?

The colonies eventually accepted the naval agreement, but there was considerable, thoughtful dissent in each of the parliaments. Common themes ran through the debates in Brisbane, Sydney, Melbourne and Adelaide. In the Queensland parliament the frontier squatter Edward

Palmer observed that if ever danger came to the colony it would come through their imperial connections, 'not through themselves at all'. 'In fact', he declared, 'that is the only way it can come ... so that instead of Britain being a shield and a protection to us from our enemies, it is a source of danger'.[21] In response William Salkeld conceded the main point of Palmer's assessment but supported the agreement because, as he had earlier explained: 'We have to incur a risk of danger over which the colonies can in no sense have control. That is a fact we cannot get away from, and we must make the best of things as they are'.[22]

Palmer spoke as 'a native of the colony' and called upon his colleagues to look upon the question in the interests of the continent. Their principal concern was with 'the arts of peace and the advancement of Australia'.[23] Another Australian-born frontiersman, Boyd Morehead, asked:

> What did England care for the colonies beyond what they were worth and what she could get out of them? What did she care for them except as an outlet for her goods? She cared nothing for them, and there was nothing in common between England and the colonies, except perhaps the relationship of some people here with their friends on the other side of the world.[24]

But the overriding concern was that as a result of the agreement the colonies would participate in the foreign policy of England. They would become what Charles Chubb, the member for Bowen, called 'a belligerent portion of the British Empire'.[25]

The agreement was endorsed by a small majority in Brisbane. It passed more readily in Sydney but the accompanying debate provoked similar criticism. The member for Northumberland, Ninian Melville, said:

> Let us not go away to fight. What have we to do with England's quarrels? What have we to do with outbursts that may occur on the continent? … If Europe should become in a blaze, what should we have to do with it?[26]

Several other members said the same sort of thing. They agreed too that the country had no dangerous neighbours, no natural enemies. There was little likelihood of an independent Australia being attacked and there was sufficient local capacity for successful home defence. But the most interesting speech was delivered by John Haynes, the member for Mudgee. Today, he declared,

> we are dealing with this question: whether we shall maintain for all time the grand advantage we have had by reason of our distance from Europe, or whether we shall give it up. Our safety in the past has been undoubtedly our distance from the troubles that centre in the old world; but to-night we are to decide whether we shall take the first step that will deprive us of that position …[27]

He believed that imperialism was embodied in the proposal 'in the most minute particle'. The agreement would set the roots of imperialism in the soil of the country. Indeed it yoked the colony to 'the juggernaut of imperialism'. 'That is our doom', he warned, and continued:

> Let a cablegram come from Europe saying that the British fleet is operating against a foreign foe in the Baltic or in the Mediterranean, and we shall have to recognise this fact, that the people of Australia will be engaged in a war on the rights or wrongs of which they have not an opportunity to express an opinion. Up to the present time the country has maintained a passive attitude, but now we are to be drawn into the troubles of Great Britain all over the world … It is recognised in Europe that we are only connected with England in a moral way, but once we remove the barrier which exists between Australia and Europe, we shall become embroiled in the troubles of that part of the world.

Haynes moved a radical amendment to the legislation calling for an international conference in London to declare that Australia and the waters of the Southern Ocean were henceforward neutral territory for all time. It was an expedient that would 'gradually get us away from involvement in European trouble'.[28] Imperial sceptics raised similar issues in the Victorian and South Australian parliaments, but they were outvoted by loyalists and no one else was ambitious enough to advocate an international conference on southern hemisphere neutrality.

In the many debates and discussions about naval defence it was widely appreciated that much more than defence was at stake. The future relations within the empire were under question at a time when the cause of imperial federation was flourishing, contemporaneous with a vigorous reassertion of colonial radicalism. The historian of Australian republicanism Mark McKenna notes that by mid-1887 the cause was suddenly back on the political agenda after an absence of more than thirty-five years. The issue of a republic was raised among all colonies, classes and cultures. It was, he observes, an integral part of colonial politics and was espoused in town and country alike. During the twenty years leading up to Federation, McKenna has identified more than fifteen republican organisations and over twenty newspapers and journals that were sympathetic to the cause.[29] Republicans dressed in many different colours. They were often activists who took up many other contemporary causes, among them socialism, land nationalisation, feminism, racial inclusion, unionism and federal union. But by definition the heart of the republican cause included a rejection of monarchy, an assertion of nationalism and a wariness if not outright hostility to continuing imperial ties, with their implication of future involvement in overseas wars.

A question that needs exploring is why men and women of the period became republicans and nationalists given the enormous intellectual and emotional attraction of Britain, the empire and the old Queen. How were some people able to snap or slip out of the crimson threads of kinship, as Henry Parkes famously called them in a speech during a colonial conference in Melbourne in 1890?[30] Close attention to a single republican may tell us more than collective generalisations. Andrew Inglis Clark was one of the most important late 19th-century republicans, although he is often overlooked in modern accounts of radical nationalism. He was a successful and dynamic attorney-general in the Tasmanian parliament between 1887 and 1897, and made a significant contribution to the drafting of the Australian Constitution. He maintained his beliefs throughout his career, amid the vicissitudes of public life both at the bar and in parliament. He was one of the very few leading colonial politicians who espoused the republican cause, unlike his close Australian-born contemporaries John Forrest, Charles Kingston, Edmund Barton and Alfred Deakin. As historian John Hirst has observed, he was the only republican among the inner group of founding fathers.[31] Why was that?

Clark's republicanism was homegrown. It is not clear if he was aware of republican movements in Sydney or if he had read JD Lang's works. Their public careers just overlapped – Clark entered the Tasmanian parliament just ten days before Lang died in 1878. The bedrock of Clark's nationalism was the strong tradition of island patriotism already well developed when he was born in 1848. Settlers had quickly come to feel at home in Tasmania, and the first generation of Tasmanian-born men and women openly expressed their love for the island, without reservation or embarrassment. There was in the community a very strong sense of place. And there was a common assumption that people would as a matter of course be forever attached to the land of their birth. Tasmania was the native soil. The young Clark would have heard these sentiments expressed many times, but he always looked beyond Tasmania. As a boy he keenly followed the fate of the North in the American Civil War and was even more engaged by the reunification of Italy. Mazzini became a lifelong inspiration and his portrait hung in Clark's library. In 1890 he visited Italy while on the way to Britain and made a special trip to Genoa to visit Mazzini's tomb, which brought forth a lyrical poem that reads in part:

Before me stood a humble edifice
Whereon with words of reverence inscribed
I read Mazzini's name.
O holy prophet of humanity!
Surely thy stainless spirit floated then
Above that time-worn structure and transfused
It with a light that came
From thee invisible; for never till
That hour a fabric built by human hands
Shone with a radiance like that which clothed
That rough and lowly pile.[32]

Two of Mazzini's themes run through Clark's writing. The first relates to the importance of place, the Italian declaring that 'The life inherent in each locality is sacred'.[33] Even more significant was the central message that the diversity of the world ensured that communities would develop distinctive cultures, habits and institutions that must eventually lead to the creation of independent nation-states. Empires, by definition, frustrated the emergence of nations and thereby obstructed the divine plan. Australia, Clark believed, would inevitably follow the trajectory Mazzini had outlined. Its distinctive environment, vast size, isolation and unique history would produce a new people whose destiny required political independence. Australia was 'emphatically and peculiarly our country and our home'. The patriot's highest duty 'to our children and to humanity' was to do all that was 'within our power to ensure the development and maturity of the nation which Providence has appointed us to create'.[34] In another poem, Clark looked forward to:

A vision of a people set free
From the bonds and the toys of the past
Never bending the head or the knee
To the shadows of rank or caste.
A people whose flag shall be void
Of all traces of sceptre or crown.[35]

Clark provided a more extensive account of his ideas in one of the most important speeches of his career, delivered to the leading politicians of Australasia at the conference on Federation in Melbourne in 1890. It is worth quoting at length. 'A nation', he explained, must have an aggregate of population:

> But that population to be a nation must be localized. It must be located within certain physical limits, and must be responsive to the influences of its physical environment. I believe that it is to such conditions we owe all the nationalities existing in the world. Where a number of living units are brought in contact with

> each other within a given physical environment, there will be produced a distinct type of life, and, in the case of nations, a distinct type of national life … In Australia we have a population which is encircled by a definite physical environment … peculiarly its own, and human nature in Australia is not going to be an exception to human nature all over the other parts of the globe. It will be influenced by its environment, and it will undoubtedly, in time, produce its definite national type of manhood in response to the action of that environment. We are proud to have sprung from the same race as the inhabitants of the British Isles. I believe, however, that it is our destiny to produce a different type of manhood from that which exists in those Islands … But I believe that the distinct type of national life, which is produced by the causes I have attempted to describe, will never come to perfect fruition, will never produce the best results without political autonomy … We are asking now for the political autonomy of United Australia, in order that that national life, which we believe will exist under those conditions, may be produced and may bear the best fruits.[36]

While Clark paid tribute to Britain in his speech he had little respect for its jurisprudence, customs and institutions. His Tasmanian environment helps explain his scepticism. During his infancy, the island was deeply involved in a struggle against the imperial government to end the transportation of convicts. His family was engaged in the campaign. And in a community where a majority of people were ex-convicts or the children of convicts, sentimental talk of filial devotion to a benign motherland found little favour. As a young man, Clark wrote of a future federation as the most favourable opportunity 'for disencumbering ourselves of institutions and customs derived from feudal Europe and which have proved themselves unsuited to Australian Democracy'.[37] He sought to avoid any attempt to base Australia's future institutions on British models because it was, he believed, 'a nation in which hereditary power and privileges abound, and where, in social intercourse *caste* ruled as virtually as in India'.[38] As an industrious, reforming attorney-general he rejected the common assumption that Australian politics operated under the Westminster system. He was hostile to the monarchy, though he often kept his views to himself. Apart from the Crown's continuing right to veto colonial legislation, the ongoing connection with the British Empire would 'necessarily continue to submit Australian politics to the influence of monarchical institutions and sentiments', including the institutional deference inherent in the monarch's power to confer knighthoods and other lesser distinctions.[39]

With his back turned on Britain, Clark looked for political models where conditions were more like those in Australia. And above all he looked to the United States and studied the republic's laws and institutions, visited there on three occasions and developed close friendships with a number of prominent Americans. Boston, not London, was his intellectual home. As a young man he was the president of an American club, the members of which met on 4 July to celebrate the Declaration of Independence. When it came to drafting the Australian Constitution, Clark's American expertise was invaluable and influenced the shaping of federal–state relations, the role of the Senate and the central importance of the High Court. His contemporaries recognised the significance of Clark's American knowledge. In his book on the making of the Australian Commonwealth, fellow politician BR Wise observed that:

> No one in Australia, not even excepting Sir Samuel Griffith, had Mr. Clark's knowledge of the constitutional history of the United States; and, when knowledge of detail is combined with zeal, its influence on a deliberative body becomes irresistible.[40]

JD Lang and AI Clark, the elder a Scottish immigrant, the younger a native-born Tasmanian, were two of the most powerful intellects of colonial Australia. Both favoured and promoted the establishment of an independent, republican nation-state. Their joint advocacy reached across the second half of the 19th century. But their distinctive and radical version of colonial patriotism remained a minority cause easily shouldered aside in the march for monarch and empire by the legion of loyalists, often known these days as British race patriots. As is often the case with lost causes, the republicans have been treated with mild, retrospective condescension. But lack of popular support does not in itself devaluate the cogency of their arguments or the acuity of their expectations. Lang looked forward to his 'coming event', although it didn't arrive in his lifetime or for a long time after. But the radical nationalists were right in their expectations. The nation-state, not empire, was the way of the future. The race patriots put their hearts and intellects behind what in the long run was a lost cause.

And what an unnecessary, profligate waste of blood and treasure resulted as a consequence. It was the fevered enthusiasm of the imperial loyalists that ensured Australia would leap immediately into the Great War, with catastrophic consequences. It was the precise result that had been dreaded by several generations of imperial sceptics. Their prophetic fear of empire proved far more prescient than the imperialists' dreams of glory, imperial federation and British race hegemony. And their repeated warnings were well known, if eschewed. They were expressed in public meetings, parliamentary speeches, books and articles. Their overwhelming concern was that the crimson threads of kinship would transform into iron chains that would drag Australia into war in Europe. It didn't happen as soon as many feared, but it turned out exactly as they had so often predicted, although few could have imagined how disastrous the result would be. Twentieth-century Australia paid a terrible and unnecessary price for cleaving to the empire. Could it have been otherwise?

Clearly the republicans thought so. As we have seen, JD Lang argued in 1870 that the Australian colonies had reached their political majority and were ready for independent statehood. Whatever the case in 1870, it was certainly true in 1901. The new Federation was far better prepared for independence than the thirteen North

American colonies had been in 1783 or any of the Latin American republics that had become independent in the ensuing decades. The same would be true of many of the colonies that gained their independence after the Second World War. Australia had a population of 4 million at the start of the 20th century. Nineteen of the world's then sovereign states had smaller populations, and many of those with more people could not have matched Australia's wealth or volume of trade. Australia and New Zealand had the highest GDP per head in the world, higher even than the United States. The country had no potentially hostile neighbours, unlike the young American republic, and, as many people argued at the time, isolation and size were strategic assets rather than liabilities. Australia depended on Britain for trade, investment and migration, but none of these were premised on continuing colonial dependence. The United States always attracted more investment and more migrants than the Australian colonies. British investors poured as much capital into Argentina as they sent to the antipodes, regardless of who was in power in Buenos Aires.

Australia no longer needed an overbearing mentor. The new federal Constitution represented a declaration of cultural independence. It showed the capacity of national leaders to borrow as much from their British heritage as necessary but no more than that, and to fuse local political practice with ideas from other sources. And intellectual and cultural interchange would have continued regardless of who held ultimate sovereignty. English ideas were not hemmed in by political borders. The Americans read English books, studied British history and shared in common cultural traditions while venerating their own institutions.

In an exchange of correspondence in 1891 with AI Clark, the veteran Victorian statesman George Higinbotham commented on the Tasmanian's draft constitution, with which he aimed to cut the constitutional ties between Britain and Australia. The older man urged the need to retain the existing forms, 'so long as we are not prepared to assume the burdens of independence'.[41] Clark on the other hand was keenly aware of the lofty condescension with which the British elite regarded the Australians and for that matter the Americans as well. He was deeply concerned in August 1900 when he heard that the imperial government had rejected the proposal in the draft constitution to make the High Court the final court of appeal and thereby bring to an end Australian access to the Privy Council. He wrote a long and detailed attack on the decision in the press in defence of the judicial independence of the Commonwealth. He observed that he expected to be opposed by two classes of people. One was made up of individuals who did not cherish 'any strong or very definite Australian sentiment on any political question'. The other consisted

> of those persons who find it difficult, if not impossible, to believe that men can be born and trained anywhere outside of the United Kingdom … who shall be equal in mental capacity to the men who occupy the judicial benches in that country. To be born and trained in either America or Australia is to such persons an immediate mark of mental inferiority.[42]

Australians like Americans were always expected to take their places 'in the second rank in the estimation of the persons who require British birth and education as the only satisfactory credentials of superiority'.[43]

Clark's frustration was palpable. It must have been the case on many occasions when he realised how powerful was the appeal among his contemporaries of sceptre and crown (see chapter 5). Clark realised more clearly than many of them the power of nationalism, but while he felt the strength of the current he misunderstood its direction in the Australian colonies. He underestimated what his near contemporary Alfred Deakin called 'the centripetal forces that draw us Australians to the Mother Country'.[44] Clark's problem had been discussed at the time of the withdrawal of British troops by an editorial writer in the Sydney paper *The Empire*, along with the belief of the members of the Victorian Parliamentary Committee that Australians were already being influenced by nationalism, 'the most subtle and pervading influence of our century', the objective of which was 'to perfect the union and autonomy of peoples of the same origin'. The Sydney writer shrewdly observed that the Victorians, like Clark and Lang, had

> overlooked the consideration that the tendency of the sentiment thus described would be not to develop a new Australian nationality, but simply to bind the Australian colonists the more closely to the people of the British Isles.[45]

We must clearly now consider the ties that bound the colonies to the imperial heartland and the forces that frustrated the expectations of the patriots.

5

The appeal of sceptre and crown

When in 1870 JD Lang was preparing his book *The Coming Event!* for publication, he was able to look back on an era when British leaders appeared to have little interest in the settler colonies and to assume they would become independent. The confederation of the Canadian provinces in 1867 seemed to beckon in that direction. The central problem was to see that when it came, separation could take place amicably. But Lang noticed two events that appeared to resist the existing tide of opinion. The first was a meeting held in London in August 1869, attended by colonial expatriates who wished to encourage the development of closer relations between empire and settler colonies. The organisation that emerged became, in 1870, the highly influential Royal Colonial Institute. The second was an article, 'England and her colonies', published in January in *Fraser's Magazine* by the editor James Anthony Froude, a leading and controversial figure in English intellectual life, a historian, novelist and essayist. Unlike many of his contemporaries he travelled widely in the colonies and became one of the most influential promoters of imperial consolidation. He visited Australia in 1885 and published his reflections in his widely read book *Oceana* the following year. The article of 1870 was a direct attack on the prevailing attitude to the colonies and the tradition of free-trade liberalism associated with Cobden and Bright, which had brought 'separation to the edge of consummation'.[1]

His central concern was with the United States, and the great waves of migration from the British Isles that removed thousands of fellow citizens from Crown and country. He feared that the settler colonies would follow the American path. If Britain continued to encourage the separation of the colonies, there was every chance that they would attempt to join the American union, because 'every one feels the benefit of belonging to a first-rate Power … An American citizen', he observed,

> is a more considerable person in the world than a member of the independent republic of Cape Town or Natal; and should the colonists take this view of their interests, and should America encourage them, what kind of future would then lie before England? Our very existence as a nation would soon depend upon the

> clemency of the Power which would have finally taken the lead from us among the English-speaking races.

The consequences would be dire. Britain would sink 'as Holland has sunk into a community of harmless traders, and leave to others the place which once we held and have lost the energy to keep'.

The essential task was 're-attaching the colonies' by providing government assistance to redirect the flood of migrants away from the United States. Consequently the emigrant, while traversing the globe, would remain English because 'he' would be on English soil 'as much as if he was in Devonshire or Yorkshire, and would remain an Englishman while the English empire lasted'. The colonies themselves would become 'feeding-places of our population' as well as 'self-supporting imperial garrisons themselves unconquerable'. With such support nothing would be able to 'check the indefinite and magnificent expansion of the English Empire'. It was a comforting image for England, but it paid scant regard to settler opinion or to what might be in the interests of the colonies themselves. Like legions of imperial spokesmen, Froude was able to assume that what was good for Britain would as a matter of course be good for the colonies as well.

But Froude's anxiety about the rising power of the United States presaged more general British concern about increasing international challenges across the following generation. If Froude had written his article a year later he would have found it necessary to respond to the dramatic developments in Europe itself with Prussia's crushing defeat of France and the emergence of a united Germany. And from 1870 until the end of the century, both Germany and the United States threatened Britain's industrial pre-eminence with vaulting economic growth and burgeoning populations. And then there was the matter of size and territorial reach. During the second half of the 19th century, both Russia and the United States expanded across vast territories, the Americans into the west towards the Pacific, the Russians into both Central and North-East Asia. There was a military problem as well. The Prussian victory over France had rewritten the textbooks, illustrating the power inherent in a well-organised, rapidly mobilised conscript army. Britain was one of the few European states that failed to introduce compulsory military service in the late 19th century.

So of those two publications of 1870 about the future of the colonies, it was Froude's article rather than Lang's book that best predicted the forward movement of opinion. The reaction against the free traders who expected and even welcomed separation, the 'Little Englanders' as they came to be known, was rapid and decisive. A major landmark was reached when Benjamin Disraeli, the leader of the Conservative Party, adopted a strong pro-empire policy, most famously in a speech in the Crystal Palace in 1872 that included a savage attack on the attitude of his liberal opponents towards the empire. For the previous forty years, he thundered, there had been no effort, 'so continuous, so subtle, supported by so much energy, and carried on with so much ability and acumen as the attempts of Liberalism to effect the disintegration of the Empire'.

Disraeli declared victory in the struggle. The desire to see the disintegration of the empire had 'entirely failed', and it had done so because of the sympathy of the colonies with the Mother Country. They had decided that the empire would not be destroyed.[2]

But the ambition to bring the colonies closer to Britain did not in itself point the way to relevant policies. The self-governing colonies were jealous guardians of their independence. Britain's decision to withdraw the imperial garrisons had broken one important connecting link. Her strong commitment to free trade precluded any use of preferential tariffs favouring the colonies. And indeed economic policy moved in the other direction. Major colonies including Canada and Victoria demanded and gained the right to levy tariffs on British goods. All these problems were highlighted when in the 1880s serious attempts were made to achieve a closer union. The Imperial Federation League was founded in Britain in 1884, and branches were established in Australia and Canada. The leading British Liberal politician WE Forster outlined the basic thinking underpinning the league. Aware of the central paradox of the constitutional position of the settler colonies, he believed that combination of independence and subordination could not long survive. It must be resolved either by disintegration of the empire or in 'complete and equal and perfect federation', which he hoped the league would achieve.[3]

The political and constitutional innovation required for a complete and perfect federation was beyond the reach of the movement, but coordination of defence was a quest that persisted when other ambitions flagged. At the time, perceptive observers appreciated that the question of defence stood at the centre of the debate about the future of the empire. Were the imperial ties a source of safety or of danger? If they could be shown beyond doubt to provide security, the 'problem of Imperial Confederation' was 'practically solved'.[4] Consequently, the crusade was part of the imperial federation movement from the beginning, vigorously promoted by a group of military and navy activists. They seized on the commitment of New South Wales to the Sudan campaign as an example of practical federation. It was a development that inspired JA Froude, who believed it would be felt all over the world. In their estimate of 'the strength, present and future, of Great Britain', the great powers had 'left the colonies unconsidered'. In the spontaneous act of the Australians,

> the great Powers would see that they would have to reckon not with a small island whose relative consequence was decreasing daily, but with a mighty empire with a capacity for unbounded expansion, her naval fortunes duly supported in the four quarters of the globe, a new England growing daily in population and in wealth with incredible speed, and all parts of it combined in a passion of patriotism, with the natural cord of affinity to which the strongest political confederacy was as a rope of straw.

And while the New South Wales contingent was only 700 strong, 'it was a specimen from an inexhaustible mine'.[5]

The second great apostle of imperial federation, John Seeley, adopted much the same argument in his widely popular and influential book *The Expansion of England*, published in 1883, warning that without the colonies Britain would be reduced to the level 'of a purely European Power looking back, as Spain does now, to the great days when she pretended to be a world-state'. He hoped that some organisation might emerge that would make 'the whole force of the Empire available in time of war'.[6] Such sentiments underpinned the foundation of the Imperial Federation League in the Australian colonies. It was vigorously promoted by the *Australian Naval and Military Gazette*, which was rebadged as *Young Australia* and became the official league journal. In fact, defence provided the bridge that led many Australians to think seriously about imperial federation.[7]

The Australian branch of the league was founded in Melbourne at a public meeting in June 1885, its beachhead the colony's anglophile upper middle class. In his study of the league, historian Charles S Blackton investigated the identity of the leading imperialists. Most were British-born and many were Anglicans holding prestigious positions. They were, he observed, well-fed, well-intentioned men of substance, who were interested in orderly progress but who 'had a dull ear for the native idiom'.[8] The league recruited the support of numerous influential newspapers and several prominent politicians. It received a significant boost in 1889 when the Canadian imperial evangelist GR Parkin embarked on a barnstorming lecture tour of the Australian colonies. While he was received with enthusiasm by committed imperialists, the feelings of opponents as well as of supporters were manifest in his public meetings. His address in Sydney in June 1889 was attended by a bevy of eminent men from politics and the judiciary. His earnest advocacy of imperial federation met with regular applause, but there were many dissidents in the audience. As reported by the *Sydney Morning Herald*, one exchange was symptomatic, with Parkin declaring 'He was mindful that his audience was a British one. (Applause, and cries of "No; it's Australian.") Very well, Australian. (Laughter and applause.)'

A little later there was further dissent, when the speaker said that with imperial federation young Australia would have a higher field for her political, spiritual and moral development than she would have if separated and by herself. He persisted with the theme:

> You say, Canada for the Canadians, and Australia for the Australians? (Great and continued applause.) He scorned the words and the thought. (Applause and groans.) Was the first voice of the colonies going to be the voice of selfishness? (Applause and interruption.) Was it going to be the wretched voice of limitation? (Applause and interruption.) He, as a Canadian was ashamed to hear an Australian say that the idea was to tie themselves within the limits of this country. (Applause and interruption.)[9]

The constant dissent foreshadowed the dramatic end to the meeting. The veteran republican David Buchanan rose to his feet the moment Parkin resumed his seat and was, the reporter observed, well received. Buchanan declared he 'could not allow such an extraordinary speech to pass without condemnation' and continued:

> The interests of Australia were the very opposite of the interests of England. (Cries of 'No' and 'Yes.') They saw nothing but the great Imperial interest. Nature had mapped out the future of this country in the form of a great consolidated Empire, independent of all other countries … He then moved, – 'That this meeting, whilst thanking Mr. Parkin for his address, is of the opinion that the natural and inevitable destiny of the Australian colonies is to unite and form amongst themselves one free and independent nation.'

The motion was seconded but the chairman refused to put it to the meeting, which resulted, in the reporter's words, in 'Uproar and cries of "Afraid"'. The meeting itself 'terminated in disorder'.[10]

There was a similar, if slightly less turbulent Hobart meeting in April 1888. It was chaired by Premier PO Fysh and attended by other leading political figures. The large audience heard a paper on the merits of imperial federation and was then presented with a formal motion which declared that imperial federation was desirable because it would 'give to all parts of the empire a voice in matters affecting all, and combine the resources of the empire for the maintenance of common interests, and the defence of common rights'.

An amendment was immediately moved by Edward Ivey, one of AI Clark's intellectual circle, protesting against the inclusion of Australia in any scheme of imperial federation. It sought to affirm the aspirations of the country for 'an Australian nationality under which to develop its institutions, and work out its destinies untrammelled by Imperial complications'. In the second part of his motion, Ivey turned to warfare, that constant concern of imperial sceptics. Viewing the situation in Europe, with every nation arming for war, he thought that if Australia were permanently united with England it would be the means of the empire 'continually embroiling her in her quarrels'. Consolidation of defence preparations was precisely the development to be avoided. Another of AI Clark's friends, FW Piesse, explained that it was that position of having a voice in England's wars 'to which they did not wish to attain'.[11] Ivey's motion, unlike Buchanan's, was put to the meeting and was narrowly lost.

The relative vigour of the imperial federation movement in the late 1880s, and its obvious elite support, stimulated a strong nationalist response. The Sydney *Bulletin* attacked in its inimitable larrikin way. A variety of writers produced essays and books promoting local patriotism. Many of their arguments drew on themes found in the work of JD Lang and AI Clark. There was the same longing for independence and the belief that loyalty belonged to the homeland, to continental Australia, not to a distant Britain. The nationalists were buoyed by the rapidly increasing percentage in the population of the native-born, and by the concomitant belief that they would give their prime loyalty to the land of their birth. Underpinning much of the advocacy was the Mazzini-derived belief that the nation-state was the natural, even the divinely ordained destiny for all the world's peoples. Closer ties with the empire were both inimical to national evolution and inherently dangerous. As so often in earlier debates, the argument was that further entanglement with the empire promised future, unnecessary involvement in foreign wars.

Nationalists were aware of Britain's history of endless conflict. The Sudan commitment was a warning of future military adventures. In an article entitled 'Australia militant' in the *Melbourne Review* in 1885, banker and man of letters HG Turner contrasted the peaceful progress in Australia with the situation in the northern hemisphere, where scarcely a year had passed that had not seen the 'dogs of war' slipped 'on some less favoured land'. He then listed all of Britain's military adventures since the end of the Napoleonic wars. He believed that 'meddlesome interference in the affairs of other countries' would lead Britain into a further succession of little wars.[12] In 1888, the radical nationalist Robert Thomson published his pamphlet *Australian Nationalism*, which he described as 'an earnest appeal to the sons of Australia in favour of the federation and independence of the states of our country'. In a chapter on imperial federation he warned that it would tie Australia 'to the fortunes of the British Empire by the iron chains of a military federation with the most warlike and warring country in existence'. And Britain's history was 'one long scene of aggression'. Her pathway round the world had been 'a track of blood'.[13]

The central question emerged again and again. Would imperial federation 'diminish the chances of war or strengthen us against foreign aggression'?[14] In an article on the future of the Australian colonies, DG Ferguson warned that it was highly probable that they would

> one day be forced into hostilities, and compelled to defend themselves against some power with which they have no quarrel, at the bidding of a few men on the other side of the world, to whom they have delegated no representative functions, and over whose actions they have not the semblance of control. The position is uniquely paradoxical. Here is a people, not under the rule of some absolute despot, but a free self-governing community, liable at any moment to be precipitated into war, to have its trade destroyed and its territory devastated – and this neither by its own act nor by the act of its representatives, nor even by unprovoked aggression.[15]

In an article titled 'An Australian protest against imperial federation', George Meudell argued that if the country 'ceased to be regarded as a dependency of the hated Mistress of the Seas', it would not require the protection of the British fleet. Australia, 'to neutralize, must first denationalize herself'. Imperial federation meant 'a retrogression to the militant *régime* from which we are emerging'.[16] Few of the critics of imperial federation were pacifists. While they argued that an independent Australia would avoid involvement in Britain's wars, they were confident that home defence would provide adequate protection from any potential threats. Many writers referred to the experience of the United States and her history of isolationism, but beyond that the whole debate turned on the question of future security and the part Britain would play in that story.

There was probably a greater range of views among proponents of empire than among their adversaries. Some imperialists conceded that adhesion to the empire increased the chance of unwanted war but accepted the risk as a necessary condition of imperial membership. Australia had received many benefits from empire and was morally obliged similarly to accept some of the accompanying costs. Gratitude was a common theme, and well-read colonists were aware of the overseas literature that emphasised the importance of the colonies to Britain's future global status. Empire loyalists took a diametrically different view of colonial Australia's long period of external peace. While nationalists referred to the fortuitous geographical isolation from the turbulent corners of the world, imperialists attributed the long-enjoyed security to the protective shield of the British Navy. And while nationalists continued to rest their case for independence on the continent's size and location, their opponents took up two opposing positions. Technology had dramatically altered the national circumstances. Steamships and the electric telegraph had brought historical isolation to an end. Australia was now tied to the world, for better or worse. The intrusion into the Pacific of the French and of the German empire in the 1880s accentuated anxieties, as did the fear of the growing Russian far-eastern fleet at Vladivostok.

The increasing tensions in Europe, and the competition for colonies and markets, were noted by both sides of the debate. Nationalists sought separatist security from the growing global instability. Imperialists looked more keenly to what they called the motherland and sought to provide what assistance they could. They applauded the dispatch of the Sudan contingent and were happy to envisage future engagements of the same kind.

But on neither side of the debate were arguments purely utilitarian. Calculation gave way to sentiment much of the time. Both nation and empire inspired devotion and emotional commitment. They were, after all, two of the most powerful contemporary causes, whose currents were felt all over the world. The empire had such pulling power, so much compacted prestige. And at the head of it all sat the monarch, in the late 19th century the old Queen, whose aura had been sedulously crafted by spectacle and ceremony. The monarchy was the fountainhead of patronage, dispensing honours all over the empire. Most Australian leaders accepted the knighthoods offered to them. Many more desired them. Many organisations sought permission to attach the term 'royal' to their titles. Republicans had nothing like it – no uniforms, no honours, no elaborate hierarchy. Loyalty to the monarchy was the single most compelling attraction of the empire, and in many imperial loyalist hearts and minds there was no conflict or contradiction between the appeal of nation and of empire.

Emotion congealed what to nationalists was an obvious fissure. Either you were an Australian or an expatriate. They thought that one must be given priority. Emotional attachment to one drained away commitment to the other. But that failed to take into account or effectively contend with a profoundly different idea of the nation. For patriots like AI Clark, the nation was bounded by geography. It was above all a place, a confined soil. For many imperial loyalists the nation was not bounded at all. The nation to which they owed loyalty was the British nation, which was a compound of race, language, history and culture. It was not a place at all or not a single fixed place. Commitment flowed out over national boundaries and knew no constraints. It was a deeply appealing vision and grew from the idea of a greater Britain which had captured the imagination of large groups in Britain itself but also in the settler dominions. It underpinned the empire until the middle of the 20th century.

A foundation text for the concept of greater Britain was written by the 24-year-old aristocrat CW Dilke, who visited Australia at the end of a world tour in 1867. It was globetrotting with high intellectual purpose. In a letter to his father while on the track, he explained that the key to his tour was to examine the condition of the 'English race' in America, New Zealand and Australia.[17] His travels confirmed his evangelical zeal concerning the destiny of that race. As he left Australia he explained to his father that he did so 'with a greater belief than I ever before possessed in its destined predominance over all other races'.[18] On his return he quickly wrote the popular book *Greater Britain*, which remained in print for many years. His preface foreshadowed the essence of his message:

> In 1866 and 1867, I followed England round the world: everywhere I was in English-speaking, or in English-governed lands. If I remarked that climate, soil, manners of life, that mixture with other peoples had modified the blood, I saw, too, that in essentials the race was always the same. The idea which in all the length of my travels has been at once my fellow and my guide – a key wherewith to unlock the hidden things of strange new lands – is a conception, however imperfect, of the grandeur of our race, already girdling the earth, which it is destined, perhaps, eventually to overspread.

Dilke ended with a clarion call: we 'must form a Greater Britain'.[19]

Greater Britain was an important book, the prelude to a large, sympathetic literature about race and empire, and an accompanying revolution in thinking about the settler colonies, not just in London but in Toronto, Wellington, Melbourne and Cape Town as well.[20] The emphasis on race was of central significance. For Dilke it underpinned every other social and cultural phenomenon. It was the elixir that fused together the British settlements and provided the irreplaceable basis for imperial federation. Unity was there in the blood. It was the role of leaders to achieve the political consummation, bringing institutional life into harmony with biology. The great migrations had not disrupted the primordial oneness. Race overrode place.

The great mid-Victorian philosopher John Stuart Mill was disturbed by Dilke's biological determinism and wrote to him after reading *Greater Britain*, observing that the young man wrote as if race and climate were the only sources of national character, whereas the 'good and bad influences of education, legislation and social circumstances' were of 'prodigiously greater efficacy'.[21]

Few members of Britain's intellectual and political elite followed Dilke's trail to the Australian colonies, but talk of blood, race, kinship and family spread widely. WE Forster looked forward to the approaching day when 'England's children' would be united with 'the mother-country, in a permanent family union'.[22] Such sentiment was ubiquitous by the end of the 19th century. But there was much calculation as well. Among British political and intellectual leaders there was a keen awareness of how much they needed the settler colonies, and of the value of the rhetoric of blood and family in countering colonial nationalism. In his 2007 study of the idea of greater Britain, Duncan Bell observed that concern about its obvious growth 'motivated urgent calls to halt, slow down, or at least redirect this dangerous process'.[23] In his highly influential book *The Expansion of England*, JR Seeley argued that the colonists must be warned of risks of independence, but also of what he assumed would be the resulting 'intellectual impoverishment'.[24] The imperialists were clearly ambitious. Seeley looked forward to the time when Canada and Australia would 'be to us as Kent and Cornwall'.[25] Sir John Cramb explained that the general aim of British imperialism was 'to give all men within its borders an English mind'.[26] Froude wanted colonists to 'remain attached to the Crown, where their well-being would be our well-being, their brains and arms our brains and arms, every acre which they could reclaim from the wilderness, so much added to English soil'.[27]

But condemnation of colonial nationalism was only a small part of pro-imperial propaganda, which was both diverse and intense, flooding out from Britain into every corner of the empire.[28] A winning theme was the limitless prospects for a greater Britain. The promise of future grandeur in Dilke's book of 1868 was picked up and repeated over and over again. It was central to the advocacy of imperial federation, GR Parkin declaring that the 'amazing spread of the race' had become the 'main fact of modern history – the one which will have the most decisive influence on the history on the future of mankind'.[29] For the true believers the consolidation of the empire was a 'vast question' upon which the whole future of the country depended. 'In magnitude', Seeley believed, this question far surpassed 'all other questions' which could be discussed in political life.[30] At times enthusiasm approached euphoria, even among earnest men of letters. In *England in the Nineteenth Century*, published in 1900, the leading historian CW Oman observed that for the previous ten years, imperial federation and racial patriotism were topics that had been 'in every mouth'. He believed that 'a well-compacted union of all the British lands would form a state that might control the whole world'. He continued in prophetic voice, 'If, as we confidently hope, they [the British lands] hold together and combine in some more or less definite federal scheme, the future of the whole world lies in the hands of the Anglo-Saxon race'.[31] It was a heady vision to present to the white colonists, and even if their participation was always likely to be in a subaltern role, it was an appealing alternative to colonial nationalism.

But majority opinion in Australia avoided the competing extremes of radical republicanism and sovereign independence on the one hand, and imperial federation on the other, while being influenced by both. The practical difficulties of projecting a realistic model of constitutional federalism proved insuperable. Sir Henry Parkes, the veteran colonial politician, observed that imperial federation was unacceptable because it could not be based on equality of the contracting parties. Opposition came as well from the Australian Natives' Association (ANA), an organisation founded in 1871 by Australian-born men in Victoria, which remained its heartland. The ANA promoted overtly nationalist causes across a wide terrain, but most substantially the federation of the colonies, white Australia and the assertion of the nation's interests in the Pacific. League spokesmen were quick to answer critics who described the organisation as anti-British or republican, arguing that it represented 'the happy medium between undesirable extremes'.[32] It did reflect the fusion of a nationalism that was directed at specific causes with loyalty to both Crown and the imperial heartland. The association supported the colonies' military adventures, officially applauding the dispatch of the Sudan contingent and coming out strongly in support of the Boer War involvement, to the extent of raising companies of volunteers.[33]

Alfred Deakin was a representative figure. Native-born like AI Clark, he was a prominent member of the Victorian colonial parliament, an early member of the ANA, an influential federalist, a leading figure in the fledgling federal parliament and, later, three times prime minister. Among his array of activities he became the president of the Victorian Imperial Federation League, which, anomalously, continued to operate long after the dissolution of the British parent branch. In his presidential address in June 1905, he delivered an eloquent statement of the ties that bound the new federal Australia to Britain:

> It is not necessary to catalogue the centripetal forces that draw us Australians to the Mother Country. The same ties of blood, sympathy, history, and tradition which make us one Commonwealth here, make the British of to-day one people everywhere. Imperial federation points to closer relations, not only with Great Britain, but with all those great dominions of hers of the same type ... As a united whole we appear none too strong to protect ourselves against those other Powers who are to-day our rivals, and may at any time become our foes. As a unit Australia, with her small population, if we stood alone, must obviously fall prey to allied aggression. Even Great Britain herself, if confined to Europe, must shrink from the high estate and commanding authority she now enjoys. All our interests, all our memories, characters, aims, and hopes of realising them pacifically must draw us closer together. Our race has its faults ... but we would be much poorer, and the world as a whole deeply impoverished, if we were scattered peoples, marching apart in segments instead of confronting destiny shoulder to shoulder.[34]

Imperial federation was not a successful cause. Enthusiasm for it waned everywhere sooner or later. But the idea of a greater Britain was another matter altogether. As many imperialists hoped, it provided a most effective counter to radical republicanism and expectations of national independence. It was clearly not imposed on the Australians from outside. Many of them were inspired by the grand vision on offer. They felt it was possible to combine local nationalism with imperial grandeur.

But the settler dominions were only independent in relation to domestic matters. They were still tied to the chariot wheels of the British state. War, peace and diplomacy were exclusively imperial matters. All the sentiment about the monarchy and the long and rich history could not disguise the fact that in matters of the greatest national importance, the dominions were captive to the imperial will. The situation in the first years of the 20th century remained as it had been in the 1880s, when EA Freeman observed that 'the fullest independence in local affairs' could not disguise the fact that in 'strictly national affairs the freest of colonies' was as 'dependent as ever' and might 'at any moment find itself plunged into a war', in the nature or location of which it had no say.[35] It was equally clear that the constantly repeated warnings of the radical nationalists that Britain was a source of danger were as pertinent as ever. Australian leaders such as Deakin who wanted to draw closer to Britain had either forgotten or disregarded the prophesies of the colonial Cassandras, whose dire premonitions were largely ignored.

Not that the problem had gone away, the upsurge of

imperial loyalty notwithstanding. The radical economist JA Hobson observed in 1909:

> To speculators upon the larger problems of history it will be a particularly interesting and delicate consideration whether our colonial nations will best consult their safety and their liberty in the future by remaining formal members of the Empire, sharing both the risks and the resources of this association, or by taking their destinies entirely into their own hands, forming their own alliances, and meeting out of their own resources the rarer risks which might attend such severance.[36]

A consideration of the future of what increasingly came to be known as 'the dominions' had to involve the sense of kinship, which meant much more in Australia than it did in Britain. We must now consider that idea of family loyalty.

6

The illusions of an imperial family

Republicans who wanted to see the settler colonies achieve independent nationhood frequently alluded to the accustomed pattern of family life. Nations, they said, were like young men who, on reaching adulthood, left the family home and went their own way. Imperialists were equally fond of familial metaphors. Britain was the motherland, the settler colonies her children. The language of affection, duty and devotion was ever-present. To what extent contemporaries could distinguish between figures of speech and the reality of international politics is hard to determine. British leaders certainly encouraged emotional attachment in the absence of demonstrable practical benefits. JA Froude believed that sentiment lay 'at the root of every powerful nationality'.[1] Lord Rosebery, a Liberal imperialist and president of the Imperial Federation League, saw the empire as a 'union in sympathy'. His like-minded colleague Sir Edward Grey believed the white settler colonies were bound to Britain not by force but 'by sentiment and affection'.[2] In a speech delivered in 1887, Joseph Chamberlain declared that 'The tie which binds us to Australia is a sentimental tie'.[3] Australian colonists were equally complicit in using the language of the hearth when illustrating the basis of their much-paraded loyalty.

Was there any harm in it? Probably there was. To the extent that it cloaked the real basis of colonial dependence, it served the interests of Britain rather than those of the dominions. Hard thought was softened by sentiment. Loyalty existed in a realm out of the reach of reason. But to what extent colonial affection was reciprocated is a pertinent question. Empires are not acquired or maintained by the soft emotions of the fireside, and talk of family hid more than it revealed. Dominion leaders were not treated as valued members of the family. Far from it. They were considered too crude and provincial to be involved in the delicate work of international diplomacy, so it was best to keep them in ignorance.

Nevertheless, Australians and the citizens of the other dominions were encouraged to believe they had a special relationship with their homeland. Shared language and customs were assumed to foster common interests. And there was the burgeoning belief in the central importance of race, more marked on the periphery than at the centre of the empire. Race and blood were thought to provide the basis for deep communion. But such talk of a brotherhood of white men was an embarrassment in a multiracial empire with a large non-European majority. The Australians rarely seemed to appreciate that India was far more important to Britain than was Australia. Britain's strategic priorities remained Europe, the Mediterranean, the Middle East and India, and the great spread and size of the empire ensured that Australian interests were far less important in London than the Australian public appreciated. Deft imperial diplomacy disguised the truth of the matter and continued to do so until well into the 20th century.

Class and, above all, status meant more to the imperial ruling class than race. Up until 1914, British politics was still dominated by the aristocracy and acceptable members of the upper-middle class. The government in power at the time of Australian Federation was led by Robert Cecil, 3rd Marquess of Salisbury. The cabinet included one duke, eight lords, one earl, two knights and several commoners with familial links to the aristocracy. A greater contrast with the men who filled the benches in the Australian parliaments would be hard to imagine. So while Deakin may have wished to advance shoulder to shoulder with his British counterparts and presumed racial brothers, there is no certainty they would have welcomed such physical intimacy with an Australian, and they certainly would not have allowed their daughters to marry one.

The profound difference in social background between the leaders of Britain and of the colonies was of real and practical importance. The social distance was almost unbridgeable. Colonial leaders had risen above their station. They would not have held high positions in Britain, but they were not necessarily deferential as such men would be expected to be if they had not gone out to or been born in the colonies. The Australians were always at a social disadvantage when dealing with imperial leaders, who characteristically had the supreme self-confidence emanating from inherited privilege. Colonial leaders faced a difficult situation. They either had to accept this effortless assumption of superiority or react against it and be dismissed as graceless upstarts. And it was the English leaders who made the rules and defined the prevailing punctilio, down to the cut of a collar, the enunciation of a vowel or the protocols of the dining table. Family the colonists might be, but they were embarrassing, underbred relations.

And the British elite were remarkably insular, their imperial reach notwithstanding. Colonial politicians probably had a much wider experience of life and had often seen more of the world. The Australians knew much more about Britain than British leaders knew about the antipodes. The typical education and training of the upper classes were so uniform and so exclusive that it was difficult for any outsider to be considered a true gentleman. When she was in South Australia as the wife of the governor, Audrey Tennyson concluded there was 'not a real gentleman or lady in the country'.[4] The leading military figure Sir Ian Hamilton made a similar comment about Australian society while visiting just before the war in 1914, writing home to his wife: 'And the people are so *commonplace*.

For Heaven's sake keep that to yourself but so far it strikes me so. They are just very ordinary middle class British – nothing more – nothing less'.[5]

The Fabian socialist Beatrice Webb visited Australia and had much the same view. The Australians were like the English middle class but if anything their manners were worse, 'the dress more pretentious and glaring and lacking in taste than with us!' As for the well-to-do women, they received an even more damning report. They lacked culture, 'charm and any kind of grace; and the richer they are the more objectionable they become'.[6] Many members of English upper classes did not like Americans either, unless they were rich heiresses. But they were not seen, as the Australians were, to be under-bred, second-rate Britons.

This attitude was examined by David Cannadine, the prominent historian of class in Britain, in his book about the empire called *Ornamentalism*. He observed that while it was true that the British overseas came from the same racial stock as the British at home, and shared skin colour and racial kinship, the metropolitans never lost the basic sense of their superiority of rank and wisdom over colonials. In the 19th century, Australians were dismissed for being Irish Catholic or the descendants of convicts, or both. Many Britons saw their settlement empire not as a great white hope but as a sociological dumping ground for the dross and detritus of the British metropolis – convicts and their progeny, poor rejects from the slums, failed professionals, indebted and scandal-blighted aristocrats. They were, Cannadine argued, 'rootless, marginal people, unable to find or take or keep a place in the metropolitan social order, or cast out from it. They were the poor whites or white trash of the time'.[7]

Superiority and condescension, even when skilfully cloaked with rarely failing politeness, were serious matters with important consequences. In the end they proved a major obstruction to imperial cooperation. The leading historian of the empire, Ronald Hyam, observed that there was much prejudice against colonials, who were thought 'swaggering, boring, impudent'. This was particularly the case with Australians. In fact, contempt for them was so great that there was never the slightest intention before the First World War of admitting them to the seats of power, despite the sweet talk about imperial fellowship.[8] The colonial secretary Lewis Harcourt, in rejecting a proposal for further cooperation, wrote in his private correspondence in 1911 that it would 'never do to *say* we are too good for them, and they are not good enough for us'. So all one could do was to pander to the 'social vanities of the new rich' until they could be convinced of the 'folly of their foibles'.[9] The secretary to the Admiralty, Sir Graham Greene, found the Australians irresponsible and thought that their 'swollen heads were bothersome'.[10] The prominent Tory politician and aristocrat Lord Hugh Cecil thought the colonial leaders 'windy-minded underbred spouters'. They were 'transoceanic mediocrities'.[11] Sir Edward Grey, the Liberal foreign secretary, was equally hostile. Having been invited to address the Victoria League in April 1908, he wrote in response:

> If I spoke my mind it would appear something like this … 'I think there is too much tendency here to slobber over the Colonies, and they are too much given to spit at us. I except Canada from this criticism, but for Australia it might be put even stronger, etc., etc.' I fear this wouldn't do.[12]

Alfred Deakin, the suavest and most intellectual of the Australians, failed to measure up even among liberal politicians who would have shared his political views. The veteran Liberal minister John Morley found mixing with the colonials at a conference in 1907 as 'the greatest bore that ever was known'. He confided in a letter to a colleague that he found Deakin intolerable, writing:

> Our robust young Colonials are apt to be frightful bores, and if you had been condemned to eat twenty meals day after day in their company, and to hear Deakin yarn away by the hour, I believe you would be as heartily glad to see their backs as I am.[13]

The liberal philosopher LT Hobhouse held a similarly dim view of colonial leaders, who were, he wrote, 'plain men of the rough-and-ready British type'. Altogether they were 'dull fellows, it is to be feared'.[14] Even young colonial Rhodes scholars failed to impress. When Colonial Office official Charles Lucas suggested recruiting young men who had been trained at British universities as a gesture in support of imperial cooperation, his minister, Lewis Harcourt, rejected the proposal, observing that despite their sojourn in Britain, the colonial graduates did not seem 'to acquire the "nameless polish" of the University'.[15]

Such dismissive views mattered. They were not confined to the Edwardian years. Similar comments were exchanged among British leaders up to and during the Second World War. This was clearly the case with Winston Churchill. He shared his contemptuous attitude with Lord Hugh Cecil, who had been the best man at his wedding. Australians, he believed, came of 'bad stock'. The historian of Anglo-Australian relations during the 1940s, David Day, observed that:

> Churchill could not help being dismissive of a country established originally as a convict colony and subsequently settled by large numbers of working-class Irish. His views would have been shared widely within Britain's ruling class, if only subconsciously, and would have exacerbated the prevailing resentment towards Australia.[16]

For all the talk of imperial cooperation, the British leaders did not really like the Australians and found their democratic manners offensive. When in Australia, Dilke confided to his father that he found democracy discomforting, 'all my *English* prejudices being aristocratic'.[17] They expected to be recipients of a double deference, firstly to themselves as they would assume at home, and secondly to Britain itself. They bridled when confronted by colonial self-confidence, which they thought was both impudent and unwarranted. Froude presents a classic case study.

When he visited Australia he mixed with the British-born upper classes and was impressed by how English society was and presumably how respectful his hosts had been. But on the boat crossing the Pacific he came across a different type of Australian altogether. He explained that he had met a younger generation of colonials:

> Those we had on board, and there were a good many of them, were of the moneyed kind, who had leisure and means and the self-sufficiency which goes along with it. Of these I liked none. They were, as a rule, vain, ignorant, underbred, without dignity, without courtesy, and with a conceit which was unbounded.

He was even more offended by a young man who was a representative of one of the great mercantile houses, who talked of Australia's boundless future and was 'so satisfied with his country and himself'. Froude was affronted all over again by the 'blandness and conviction' with which this young man expressed his patriotism, which 'would have been entertaining if it had not been so absurd'.[18] Hatred is not too strong a word to describe Froude's attitude to the young Australians. And he was an apostle of imperial federation.

Dilke and Froude had at least been in Australia. That was unusual. Despite the ease of international travel for the well off in the late 19th century, few upper-class English men or women actually travelled to the antipodes, even when they were enthusiasts for closer imperial engagement. Was there any real concern for what might have been in the best interest of the Australians? The free-trade liberals had assumed that Canada and Australia would follow the example of the United States and might indeed benefit as a result. There is little comparable comment in imperial federation literature. The assumption seemed to be that the colonies would be better off if they were closer to Britain. The possible advantages of independence were rarely canvassed.

This raises the question of why the British leaders took new interest in the settler colonies from 1870 onwards, and why then? Froude's article of 1870 prefigured much of what was to follow. The colonies, he argued, would help preserve Britain's status as a great power threatened by rivals. During the next generation such anxieties proliferated even while the empire reached its greatest extent. One of the problems facing the advocates of imperial federation was that it was not entirely clear what the dominions were expected to do. They did not provide Britain with the vast territorial expanse of the United States or Russia, even if you added Australia and Canada to a list of English-speaking territories. Contiguity and control were what really mattered. Free trade gave Britain access to whatever colonial resources she wanted at market prices, and the local traders and parliaments were never going to accept less. British financiers had easy access to the money markets and to capital-hungry governments. Froude and many more after him had fantasies of mass migration to the dominions, but governments could do little to counter the more attractive prospects presented by the United States. And the colonial parliaments were not going to surrender their jealously guarded control over migration. So what was it that attracted so many leading figures to the idea of imperial federation? There was, as might be expected, much more to it than sentimental talk about family loyalty and close kinship.

There is a consensus now about Britain's decline relative to the United States, Germany and Russia. It began in the 1870s, Ronald Hyam writing that the empire 'carried the sentence of death within itself from at least the 1890s, perhaps even from the 1870s …'[19] Imperial federation was a response to the consequent growth of pessimism, to the belief, apparent in Froude's article of that year, that Britain faced a diminished, shrunken future, like her one-time imperial rivals Holland, Portugal and Spain. They were minatory models.

Between 1870 and 1914, Britain faced economic challenge from the rapidly industrialising Germany and above all the United States. There was also rivalry with France and Germany in Africa and the Pacific, and with Russia in Central Asia. But there was a distinctive, inimitable problem relating to military power. There were a few passing scares about the navy but Britain was able to maintain her supremacy at sea and preserve the axiomatic doctrine of the two-power ascendancy by which the Royal Navy could outgun the second- and third-ranked naval powers. But when it came to the army it was a different story altogether. There were a series of interlocking, compounding problems. There was the obvious difficulty of garrisoning the vast empire, including the many naval installations and coaling stations scattered around the edges of the world's oceans. The withdrawal of the last regiments from the dominions in 1870 was an obvious response to the more general problem. In other parts of the empire, particularly around the Indian and Pacific oceans, the Indian army was employed, largely funded out of local revenue and not by the British Treasury. But there were problems with expanding its size, despite the huge domestic population. There was an understanding, pervasive since the Indian Mutiny, that at least one-third of the troops must be British.

The problem of a restive empire was manageable while Britain commanded the seas and could move troops quickly around the world, creating an illusion of military potency. But when it came to Europe it was a different story. Britain faced great difficulties if her leaders wanted to influence the continental balance of power. There was much debate about that, but involvement was required if Britain wanted to maintain her status as a great power. This is where the large problems bit deeply. It's where numbers really mattered and could not be avoided.

The military map of Europe was transformed after the German defeat of France in 1870. Large conscript armies, now mobile on proliferating rail networks, became the new standard. All the continental countries with the exception of the Netherlands adopted conscription, and at least on paper had huge armies totally overshadowing British forces available for home defence. Compounding the difficulty was Britain's continuing commitment to a volunteer army, which lasted until as late as 1916. There was an ancestral suspicion of a standing army and a liberal hostility to conscription, with its authoritarian overtones.

It was a source of both pride and frustration among military planners.

Sir Ian Hamilton, who later commanded the Allied forces in the Gallipoli campaign, declared in 1910 that war was 'essentially the triumph … of one will over another weaker will'. Volunteers had the upper hand because they were animated by a superior moral force. This was an ideal that had 'guided British theory and practice for centuries'.[20] The frustration was voiced by another military leader with Australian connections, Major General Sir Edward Hutton, who had commanded the military forces in New South Wales during the 1890s and those of the Commonwealth after Federation. He calculated in 1905 that Britain required a field army of 500 000 men, far in excess of what was available at the time. He wondered where they would come from, because:

> The Anglo-Saxon race has declared against conscription upon the European model, and it is impracticable under the conditions now prevailing to expect any change in public feeling … It is, at any rate, useless to suppose that by any possible process a regular or standing army can be created or maintained which will provide the troops shown to be necessary.[21]

With his Australian experience, however, Hutton knew where to turn. Like military planners for at least a generation, he looked rapaciously at the young men in the dominions. Almost every assessment of British military strength written from the 1890s onwards had counted the military forces that might be drawn from overseas British populations quite regardless of the fact that at the time opinion in the dominions was strongly against committing even small armed forces for overseas service. And while the language was all about mutual defence, the inescapable reality was that what Britain needed, and wanted, was soldiers for conflict in Europe. And the demands of modern warfare meant that what was really required were contingents of an agreed size, with men armed and trained in order to be easily inserted into the imperial army. It was to be a one-way traffic with troop movements in a single direction. At no point did the British military planners think their regiments would be required to defend the dominions. Canada was seen to be indefensible in the event of conflict with the United States. The strategic assessment was that Australia and New Zealand were not threatened by anyone and that the worst that might happen would be incursions by small raiding parties. The major port cities were easily defended against attack from the sea, and the colonial governments had developed effective defensive fortifications.

The New South Wales contingent committed to the Sudan in 1885 was, as it turned out, impeccably timed, although this did not seem to be apparent to the politicians in Sydney. It was not that Britain wanted, let alone needed, the colonial involvement, but it took place when Britain was in the middle of an intense debate about military capacity and preparedness. Consequently, it was seized upon by military planners and defence commentators for special attention, not for the brief adventure itself but for what it might mean in the future. It was thought to be more important in Britain than it was in the colonies, where after a year or two it was more often ridiculed than admired. The prominent Anglo-Irish historian WEH Lecky addressed the Imperial Institute in 1893 and declared that it was unspeakably important to the future of the world that the British race 'through the ages to come, should cling as closely as possible together'. He recalled the Sudan campaign, observing: 'those who have understood the significance of that memorable incident in our recent history – the despatch of Australian troops to fight our battles in the Soudan – may perceive that there is at least a possibility of a still closer and more beneficial union …'[22]

The leading politician Joseph Chamberlain referred to the same event in a speech on relations with the United States and the colonies in April 1888, in which he expressed the hope that Canada, South Africa and Australia would not follow the American path to independence. He told his audience how encouraged he was by the involvement of the New South Wales troops in the Sudan campaign.[23] As far back as 1870, Froude had described military assistance from Greater Britain as derived 'from an inexhaustible mine'.[24]

CW Dilke became a major figure in the debate about military power and the empire in the 1890s after he was forced to resign from Gladstone's cabinet following his involvement in a scandalous divorce case. He returned to his interest in Australia with the publication of a new book, *The Problems of Greater Britain*, in 1890. He was one of an influential group of activists who agitated about the need to both reform and greatly expand the British army. He observed that the empire stood at 'the top of almost every scale' by which powers were estimated, except its 'military strength in land forces'.[25] He argued that the small size of the army in Britain itself meant that a large percentage of the fleet had to be kept in home waters to deter invasion. And that mattered, because the Empire, he believed, was about to face challenges that would determine whether it had work to do in the world and whether it had the strength to do it.

Such questions, Dilke thought, were put to nations as to men 'in the form of struggle and conflict'.[26] So the time had come for welding together all the military forces of the empire, including both the Indian army and those of the self-governing colonies, 'into one great force'. What was required was to strengthen the sentiment 'of common nationality and of racial patriotism'.[27] He hoped that the British overseas would willingly defend the British homeland even when they were not threatened themselves. He had thought in 1867 that the fear of conquest of the Australian colonies if left to themselves was 'on the face of it ridiculous'.[28] And he had much the same view in 1890, pointing out the logistical difficulties facing any would-be invader of the continent. But he held out the hope that the colonists would rally behind the motherland, writing that 'We think we may safely assume that Englishmen, wherever they live, will lay down their lives, if need be, to protect English homes, both those of the Old Country and of the New Englands beyond the seas ...'[29]

The problem of how to knit the empire more closely together remained, having exercised the best minds in the country, but the closer union for the purposes of defence was 'well within view'. Dilke's solution was both simple and audacious. 'War', he wrote, 'would rapidly bring it into shape'.[30] It would be a war where colonial troops would fight to protect English homes rather than the reverse situation. And presumably any war would do, regardless of where it was fought, who it was against and why conflict broke out. It clearly didn't matter whether the dominions had any direct interest in the conflict. Brotherly engagement in battle and sacrificial sharing were what was needed to tighten the bonds of empire. Dilke must have written the relevant passage shortly before the outbreak of war in South Africa.

At the time, Dilke, while influential, sat on the backbenches in the Commons with little prospect of returning to office. His one-time colleague and close friend Joseph Chamberlain was a leading member of the government who, to the surprise of many observers, had chosen to become colonial secretary, hitherto a ministry of little prestige. He held the position from 1895 to 1903. His increasingly pressing interest in the empire was stimulated by the work of John Seeley, and he became a keen advocate of imperial federation who looked upon separation 'as the greatest calamity that could befall us'. He had no doubt that the colonists would willingly choose empire over nation and be better off for the choice. They must feel, he announced, that 'no separate existence, however splendid, could compare with that which they enjoy equally with ourselves as joint heirs of all the traditions of the past, and joint partakers of all the influence, resources, and power of the British Empire'.[31]

He was less forthcoming about the imperial propensity for war and his hope that the dominions would share the burden of perpetual conflict. In a speech to the Royal Colonial Institute in 1897, he explained that ruling the empire involved heavy responsibility because 'In the wide dominions of the Queen the doors of the temple of Janus are never closed, and it is a gigantic task that we have undertaken when we have determined to wield the sceptre of empire'.[32]

Chamberlain believed that there were two avenues along which to pursue the consolidation of the empire. Trade and defence were the pertinent points that had to be prominently borne in mind. Of the two, defence cooperation was much easier to achieve, as Chamberlain himself found out when he tried to implement a policy of tariff reform in 1903 and resigned from the government as a result. The orthodoxy of free trade was far too deeply entrenched to be easily overturned. Perhaps even more problematic was the commitment of the dominions to protective tariffs, both as sources of revenue and for the encouragement of fledgling industries often in competition with British industry. Neither Britain nor the dominions were ready for radical reform of trade policy.

The way to defence cooperation was much smoother and the problem more pressing. With war approaching during 1899 against the Dutch republics of Transvaal and the Orange Free State, Chamberlain sought military commitments from the dominions, suggesting that they should be made in such a way as to appear spontaneous. All six Australian colonies offered troops, as did Canada and

New Zealand. Chamberlain's motivation has been often discussed, but several things are clear. His objective was political rather than military. It is unlikely that, before the war, he envisaged needing colonial troops to defeat the two small republics. The colonial contribution would be useful in the inevitable debates in Britain, particularly as the infamous Jameson Raid into the Transvaal of 1895–96 was still fresh in the public's mind and Chamberlain's culpability remained open to debate. The involvement of colonial detachments, it was hoped, would be noted in Europe, where Britain's military weakness was a matter for common discussion. But Chamberlain was playing a more devious hand, and his objective reached far beyond the immediate crisis. Like his confidant Dilke, he wanted to use war to bind the dominions securely and permanently to the empire and thereby to have ready access to their potential military manpower. On the eve of the war, a company of New South Wales cavalry that was visiting Britain paraded through London. Chamberlain's biographer JL Garvin noted that he was deeply moved and felt that in that moment 'his career as Colonial Minister had a significance bringing his life to a climax'. He was equally delighted when pledges of support flowed in from the dominions. The involvement of the Australians was 'felt by him as not only part of his pride but part of his life'.

The grooming of the Australians had been highly successful and pointed to objectives beyond victory in South Africa.[33] It was an extraordinary achievement of British diplomacy to receive the military support of the six Australian colonies, New Zealand and Canada (despite the hostility of the French Canadians). The Australians and New Zealanders competed with one another to display their loyalty and to be the first to land troops in South Africa. Supporters of imperial federation were ecstatic. The secretary of state for war, the Marquess of Lansdowne, declared in a speech in November 1899 that the participation of the colonies in the war 'was unprecedented in the history of the Empire'. It was proof 'that "Greater Britain" was no empty phrase'.[34] Imperial military planners looked on, believing that the experience gained in South Africa would indicate 'the best methods of organising and utilising Colonial troops for Imperial needs'.[35]

The radical economist John Hobson watched developments from the other side of the debate, observing in 1901 that imperial statesmen were openly boasting that involvement in the war in South Africa – what he called their 'confederacy in bloodshed' – had 'annealed the colonies to the mother country'.[36] While Hobson was one of the most prominent critics of the war, his assessment of the mood among the pro-war party was apposite. Chamberlain made no secret of what he thought were the benefits resulting from the colonial involvement. In a speech delivered after the war in August 1902, he referred to the loyal sentiments that held the empire together and the need to overwhelm colonial nationalism. Indeed, the first duty of the new century was

> to confirm these loyal sentiments and to substitute in every part of the Empire broad Imperial patriotism for the provincial spirit which tends to separation and

> disruption. In performance of that duty, the war, much as we may regret it, has greatly assisted us; in fact, even for our own losses and sacrifices, great as they have been, there is some compensation to be found in the fact that the war has brought the Empire closer together.

Sacrifice and devotion, he confided, which have 'cemented our union in blood and tears must not now be suffered to weaken'.[37]

Chamberlain had influential support. The Liberal imperialist Lord Rosebery believed that colonial participation was the vital feature of the war, writing in January 1900 that despite the recent reverses, Britain had purchased a united Empire that would be 'henceforth a supreme factor in the balance of the world'.[38] In an article of 1900 on the military forces of the colonies, commentator JF Owen believed that the bonds between Britain and the colonies would for the future 'be doubly cemented by the blood of their sons shed, side by side, for the defence of the flag so dear to both'. Britain and her 'stout children' had been 'drawn to closer union by common danger overcome'.[39] In his book *The Great Boer War*, Arthur Conan Doyle declared that 'On the plains of South Africa, in common danger and in common privation, the blood brotherhood of the Empire was sealed'. In the midst of the war 'the nation was assured of its unity and learned for all time that blood is stronger to bind than salt water is to part'.[40]

And so the Australian colonies went collectively to war in the way that all those republicans and imperial sceptics had been predicting for half a century. But the experience did not, as they surmised it would, lead to a rupture with Britain. Quite the contrary. There were critics of the involvement and those who reminded the community of their astute foreboding, but there was an upsurge of imperial enthusiasm at the time that persisted after the end of the war in 1902. Many Australians were excited by the experience of war, at least when seen from afar. It was a dark and dangerous legacy for the young Federation to carry into the new century.

7

Australia's soldiers of the Queen

War dominated Australian public life in the closing months of 1899. Fighting broke out on 11 October when the Boer army pushed outward into both Natal and the Cape Colony. All local newspapers carried extensive telegraphic reports of the fighting. Expectations of early British victories led to sanguine accounts of the first encounters from highly partisan English papers and press agencies. But within a few weeks the early optimism was overtaken by news of Boer successes. British garrisons at Ladysmith, Mafeking and Kimberley were besieged, and in the middle of December the imperial army suffered three serious defeats in a week. Well-known and respected generals and famous regiments had been humiliated by the Boer farmers. The so-called 'Black Week' of 10–17 December was a devastating blow to British prestige and to the standing of the army in particular. During those early days of the war, the Australian contingents were at sea, having left Australia in the last days of October and the first week of November. Many of the men had been impatient to leave, believing that with such seemingly uneven protagonists the war might even be over by the time their ships arrived on the far side of the Indian Ocean.

Local preparations competed with South African events for space in the colonial papers. Every step towards war was detailed. Debates in the six parliaments that committed the colonies to intervention were well covered. The following recruitment of the contingents and their often rudimentary training were reported, along with the many social gatherings to farewell local boys as they left small rural communities and provincial towns to travel to the cities and join their future comrades. But no previous event could compete with the spectacular public carnivals that farewelled the contingents from the docks of the capital cities and from Newcastle and Launceston as well. Newspaper reports, edging on the euphoric, establish that most reporters were swept up in the collective enthusiasm.

Australians had discovered that war was exciting, particularly when the action was far away and leaders from all walks of life proclaimed the cause an honourable one. Australia, the Melbourne *Argus* declared, was a young community 'just awakened by the call to arms'.[1] The sheer size of the crowds was significant, even when attendance was greatly enhanced by the common declaration of public holidays. The consensus was that despite the difficulty of estimating the throngs that lined the routes from camp to pier, such public gatherings had never before been seen. The streets were full and spectators watched from every possible vantage point, crowding onto verandahs and jostling for a place at every strategic window. In Melbourne the *Argus* thought the demonstration 'magnificently impressive', and estimated that at least 250 000 had come out to see the men leave.[2] And the behaviour of the crowds suggested that any sceptics, or merely curious onlookers, were vastly outnumbered by the enthusiasts. Numerous observers thought the cheering overwhelming. The reporter for the Adelaide *Advertiser* declared that 'never in the history of South Australia' had 'so mighty a throng gathered in the streets'. There was no doubt about the popular mood; the cheering was 'something to be remembered for years'.[3]

When the band played the popular tune 'Soldiers of the Queen', the crowd was roused to 'a high pitch of excitement'. Bands all over the country performed it many times during those weeks and it appears to have been well enough known for people in the crowds to break out singing its pugnacious lyrics:

Britons once did loyally declaim
About the way we ruled the waves,
Every Briton's song was just the same
When singing of her soldier-braves.
All the world had heard it –
Wondered why we sang,
And some have learned the reason why –

But we're not forgetting it,
And we're not letting it
Fade away and gradually die,
Fade away and gradually die.
So when we say that England's master
Remember who has made her so.
It's the soldiers of the Queen, my lads
Who've been, my lads, who've seen, my lads
In the fight for England's glory, lads,
When we've had to show them what we mean:
And when we say we've always won
And when they ask us how it's done
We'll proudly point to every one
Of England's soldiers of the Queen.

The huge crowds themselves swelled patriotic fervour and greatly boosted the morale of empire loyalists. Many in the crowds may have been more interested in the spectacle than in the politics of the occasion, or were convinced that they were witnessing events of great historical importance. But the *Sydney Morning Herald* asserted that 'enthusiasm of so genuine a character' was infused with 'love of the Sovereign and pride of the race'.[4] In Melbourne the *Argus* declared that for the first time in the history of Victoria 'the thrill of patriotism vibrated through the nerves of the people'.[5] At the official lunch for the detachments embarking from Newcastle, the New South Wales colonial secretary, John See, attributed the enthusiasm to the fact that,

> we knew and felt that we belonged to and were part of the good old mother-land. (Cheers.) ... But more than that, it was the desire to show the people of the whole world that New South Wales, though so far removed, had still the same aspirations and desires in regard to the maintenance of the integrity of the Empire as had Great Britain itself.

Meanwhile, the local Anglican bishop sanctified the soldiers, telling his fellow guests that the men of the contingent poised to depart 'had actually consecrated the streets of Newcastle by having trodden them with the foot of loyalty and patriotism'.[6]

All over the country leading citizens called meetings to raise money for what were known as patriotic funds, designed to provide support for wounded and disabled veterans and for the wives and children of men who did not return. It was seen as the cause that would allow prosperous citizens to make a contribution to the war effort and would, more particularly, tap into the energy and enthusiasm of their wives and daughters. On the day of the departure of the first New South Wales contingent, a large meeting at the Town Hall launched the local fund and, as the *Herald* correspondent observed: 'Every loving reference to the mother country evoked thunderous applause; the mere mention of the fact that there were some who would question at this stage the rights of England in her trouble with the Transvaal induced hearty groaning'.[7]

The popularity of 'Soldiers of the Queen' was an intimation of the central role played by the monarchy in bolstering colonial support for the imperial cause. The old Queen was a diplomatic and political asset of immense importance, and was wielded by British leaders with the deftest cynicism. When the New South Wales parliament agreed to send the first contingent to South Africa, the governor, Lord Beauchamp, sent a secret telegram to Secretary of State for the Colonies Joseph Chamberlain suggesting 'that spontaneous expression of thanks from H.M. the Queen for troops going to S. Africa would be very deeply appreciated in Australia'.[8] Chamberlain immediately drafted an appropriate telegram in the Queen's name and sent it back to the colonies. The so-called spontaneous regal telegram congratulated the colonists for their equally fictitious spontaneous offer of troops. The Queensland premier, JR Dickson, who had been the first Australian leader to commit a detachment, rose in the Legislative Assembly a week before the first departure and triumphantly read the message in question, which had been sent simultaneously to all the Australian colonies and to New Zealand: 'Her Majesty the Queen desires to thank the people of the colonies in Australasia for their striking manifestation of loyalty and patriotism in their voluntary offers to send troops to co-operate with Her Majesty's Imperial forces in maintaining her position and the rights of British subjects in South Africa'.[9]

Dickson introduced the debate on the commitment to South Africa with a motion that the House 'renews the assurance of its loyalty and devotion to the Throne and Person of Her Most Gracious Majesty the Queen'. The war itself was the Queen's war because she had to assert her authority in South Africa, 'if that authority is to remain paramount for all time'.[10] The other colonial governments played the same royal card when motions were proposed to dispatch the troops. The wording was so crafted as to gain maximum advantage from the prestige of the Crown. In Tasmania, where there was a measure of reluctance towards becoming involved, Premier Sir Edward Braddon introduced the subject by moving the following resolution: 'This House desires to express its loyalty and devotion to Her Majesty the Queen, and sympathises with Her Majesty and the Imperial Government at the rising in South Africa …'[11]

In Victoria the premier, Sir George Turner, moved a similar motion declaring that the House desired to express 'its loyalty and devotion' to the Queen and its sympathy 'in the difficulties that have arisen in South Africa'.[12] The fulsome declarations of loyalty placed opponents of involvement in a difficult position. They had to declare that they were as loyal as anyone else despite their stand on the matter. Any suggestion of disloyalty would attract derision and condemnation, and was a heavy political burden to carry at a time when the prestige of the monarchy was at its apogee.

Yet many members of the parliaments did speak out against the South African venture, and perhaps the most striking feature of the national debate was the seriousness with which it was conducted. Supporters and opponents alike appreciated the importance of the decision for war and the unprecedented character of the actions that were being contested. They knew they were making history. As a result, the question was debated with earnest interest in the six parliaments and the twelve chambers. A large number of members rose to speak. The printed parliamentary debates represent one of the fullest records we have relating to opinion about war and peace, about nation and empire and the future of Australia's place in the world. Themes that had coursed through public debate for the previous fifty years re-emerged, revivified by the imminence of conflict.

The war party carried the debate everywhere, despite often vigorous and challenging opposition. Perhaps a quarter of the members had some doubts about the venture. They questioned the arbitrary way the decision for war had been made; they had serious doubts about the cost to challenged budgets. Some support was grudging and was given because it was thought that irreversible commitments had already been made by the time the debate took place. In the smaller colonies support was forthcoming because it was felt that otherwise they would be left behind and become no more than spectators to the national crusade at a time when impending Federation foreshadowed united endeavour. Perhaps a tenth of members had principled objections to the military adventure, but it is possible there were more among the men who didn't speak in the debates. Opposition was not a popular stand to take and was politically dangerous in the early months of the war, leading to social opprobrium and the threat of personal violence.

The leaders of the war party spoke with assured authority. They were leading figures in the public life of their respective colonies. Several of them were knights of the realm; others had distinguished careers in business or the professions. They were aware that they represented respectable opinion, that their sentiments could be heard in the gentlemen's clubs and around the glittering tables of society's leading hostesses. They had the often vociferous support of the leading newspapers and most of the churches. Editorials and sermons sang the praises of empire, suggesting that opponents of war were disloyal to the point of treason. Uncritical support for the imperial government had the appearance of common sense. Australians far and wide were proud of the great achievements of the colonial project. It was a simple move to attribute their success to the empire, to put the emphasis on the transplanted and imported rather than on the homegrown, and to doubt that the impending Federation could survive on its own.

Sentiment swayed more supporters in the direction of the war than anything else, in a manner that would have warmed the heart of a generation of British proponents of imperial federation. It was what Froude had advocated in 1870, and many other activists had followed in his path. People responded instantly and emotionally, and were grateful that Australia was being invited to become involved in grand imperial strategy and take up the banner of the Queen. The simplest reason for loyalty was that many colonists saw themselves as English, residence in the antipodes notwithstanding. At the end of the 19th century, many of the leaders in all walks of life had been born and grown up in the British Isles. The location of their birth was more important to them than their place of residence. A clear majority of the population in 1901 had been born in Australia and very few of them had ever been overseas, but the appeal of the old country was still a powerful force, enhanced by education both within the classroom and beyond. British literature and history continued to exert enormous intellectual and emotional attraction among educated colonists, who continued to think of Britain as home until well into the 20th century.

The idea of family was another powerful agent of attraction. It was not just a matter of Australians having family members in the United Kingdom, although there were many who did. It had much wider and more general application. One of the most vital forces at work, as we have already seen, was the idea that the empire itself was a family. The metaphor was constantly and casually slipped into speeches without any embarrassment or felt necessity to pause to provide explanation or justification. It was clearly taken for granted. The great difficulties of explaining how it could really apply in an empire with a large non-European majority rarely got in the way of the imperial enthusiasm. What gave greater momentum to the idea of an empire of kinship were the linked concepts of race and blood. At the time, the belief in blood relationship extended far beyond actual kin to the whole 'British race'. It was another concept that was ubiquitous in its reach, and speakers clearly meant more than a common sense of identity. Racial ideas, ascendant at the turn of the 20th century, suggested a much more visceral, biological relationship between members of the same race that distinguished them from all other members of humankind. Taken to extremes, it meant that British distinction and achievement were due to inherited racial characteristics. So a mere change of address could not free the colonists from their British heritage. They carried it in their blood. Their loyalty to Britain was instinctive and unavoidable. The new world and distinctive environment could not, by themselves, compete with the pull of heredity.

It was here that the essence of nationalism was in question. It was clearly one of the most dynamic forces in the world at the time of Australian Federation, agitating the life of all the great empires. Nationalists everywhere looked forward to the eventual creation of sovereign states congruent with the claimed historical territory of captive nations. To a large extent that process was consummated during the 20th century. This was the tradition that inspired Australian patriots, but there were such ambivalent attitudes to empire that there could be no simple transition from empire to nation. Colonial nationalism was tragically bifurcated. For many colonists their nationalist aspirations reached beyond the continental borders to the large scattered territories occupied by what they termed the English or British race.

The great Australian historian Keith Hancock observed in 1930 that among Australians of his and his parents' generation, 'pride of race counted for more than love of country'.[13] And where it really mattered was when Australians had to decide on matters of peace and war. Were local forces recruited to defend the continental homeland or did they have responsibility for the empire as a whole? Was it possible to distinguish between Australian interests and those of the empire? Was a challenge to the empire anywhere in the world also a challenge to Australia? Did Australia need to accept responsibility for not just the physical integrity of the empire but even its reputation and standing in the world? Was a challenge to Britain's prestige also a threat to Australia? Edmund Barton put the case for empire with admirable succinctness in the federal parliament when he declared 'the Empire is one nation, and if so much as one quarter of the Empire is attacked so is another'.[14] These were questions that were woven through every debate about the commitment to South Africa.

Why, the nationalists asked, should Australia become involved so far away in a country they knew little about and fight against people who could never present a threat to continental Australia? In reply, the promoters of intervention went far beyond their sentimental attachment to crown and sceptre, and developed a rationale of considerable density. The leading argument was that Australia had throughout its growth and development been shielded from possible enemies by the British fleet. Not only was it appropriate to acknowledge that debt but also to give something back in return. But there was more to it than that. Australia was still dependent on British protection and could not seriously rely upon its meagre forces, which in no way matched the vast empty continent over which the new federal government would claim sovereignty on the first day of the new century. Commitment to Britain in 1899 would build up goodwill in London which might be drawn on in future conflicts. And Britain's prestige mattered directly to Australia. It was being challenged by the two Boer republics as the world looked on. The comparative smallness of these challengers made the need to prevail even more imperative. Britain's military power, already regarded sceptically in Europe, was facing a serious challenge. The widespread hostility to Britain as a result of the war led loyal Australians to rally even more enthusiastically to the flag. And the control of the Cape remained a matter of concern among colonists, given that it bestrode what continued to be busy sea lanes to India and Australia, despite the importance of the Suez Canal.

Supporters of the war were willing to accept at face value the justification for Britain's onslaught on the small landlocked republics. They saw no need to question the veracity of press reports coming from London. It was clear that many colonists had unchallenged trust in whatever imperial leaders did or said. Their social eminence was seen as a guarantee of integrity and honesty, so Australians accepted the vigorous anti-Boer campaigns of extremely dubious provenance. The many stories of ill-treatment in the Transvaal of the foreign workers – or uitlanders, as they were known – were recycled by colonial politicians. Some of them displayed a wide-eyed innocence in their attitude to British wartime propaganda, refusing to accept the possibility that imperial politicians and officials were capable of duplicity or of ruthless brutality. A second leg of the imperial case for intervention was that a British administration would deal more liberally than the Boers with the Africans and members of the Indian diaspora. It was a major factor in winning and holding the support of British liberals, although never fulfilled after the Boer defeat. It does not seem that it played any role in mobilising colonial support for the war, however.

Of the great number of speakers on the questions of nation, war and empire, the most interesting to a modern audience are those politicians who were prominent members of the colonial legislatures who then took office in the new federal parliament. Edmund Barton, Charles Kingston and John Forrest were Australian-born contemporaries of AI Clark, but unlike him made the transition from colonial to national politics. Barton was the first prime minister, Forrest was the inaugural Minister for Defence and Kingston was Minister for Trade and Customs. Each man gave strong support to the South African venture in the two political arenas, colonial and federal. During a debate in the new Australian parliament on a defence bill, Forrest reacted to the taunt that he was 'too imperialistic', declaring:

> I am proud to say I am Imperialistic, in the sense that I believe in Australia being as closely allied as is possible to the mother country. I take this view for the very good reason that I appreciate the generous action of the mother country towards us, and for the further reason – that I believe that it is to our interest to for ever remain in the closest bonds of union and affection with the old country ... I believe that the people of the mother country are our best and surest friends. They have proved to be in the past, and therefore, I am firmly convinced that, in assisting any movement that will promote the advantages of the Empire, I am doing that which is best for Australia. After all, we must never forget we are bone of their bone, and that 'our fate and theirs for good or ill are woven threads.'[15]

As premier of Western Australia, Forrest had committed troops as a gesture of 'sympathy and loyalty'. And it went much further than that. He clearly thought of Australia not as an emergent nation-state but as merely part of the British nation, observing that 'if we value our being part of a great and mighty nation in time of peace', then Australians must be ready 'in time of war to share the vicissitudes of that nation'. And the support was to be uncritical, as shown in an exchange in parliament with FCB Vosper, the member for Coolgardie, who said that the colonists 'knew nothing about the justice or injustice' of the impending war. Forrest interjected, calling out: 'We do not want to know'. Vosper responded by observing that he and his colleagues knew little about the merits of the case, to which Forrest replied: 'You are arguing that we do not belong to the Empire'.[16]

Barton adopted the same uncritical support almost as a matter of honour, declaring that when Britain was at war it was the moment to pronounce the motto 'The Empire, right or wrong'. It was, he told the New South Wales parliament, the attitude taken by the great majority of the inhabitants of the Empire.[17] At the time he was a colonial backbencher. But he repeated the sentiments much more portentously when prime minister of the country, explaining that he understood the attitude of the man who said he was prepared to 'fight for the flag of the Empire, utterly regardless of whether the policy of the Government is right or wrong. That', he declared, 'is the position we should all take up in these matters'.[18] Underlying the uncritical stance was a naively trusting attitude towards the imperial authorities, whose decisions should be supported and followed, as he explained in the Legislative Assembly in Sydney:

> Whether the one party to the dispute or the other is in the right is scarcely now the question. We may be quite sure of this, that although it is impossible for colonies such as these to be consulted, the wisdom and intelligence of the Imperial Government and Parliament may be relied upon by those of the same blood who belong to the same race.[19]

Kingston was asked in debate if he supported the principle of 'my country, right or wrong'. He replied: 'I hold that view. May my country ever be in the right; but my country, right or wrong!'[20]

Once again the Australians responded to the call of blood and race, to what Barton called 'our own kith and kin and our own flesh and blood'. It would seem that many of the men of this generation could not imagine an Australia unattached to empire. Barton called on the federal parliament to recognise the nation's responsibility to the empire, 'so long as we remain part of it, and I hope that will be through all the days of my sons and my sons' sons, and through all our time on this earth'.[21]

Much the same spirit was apparent in July 1900, when the New South Wales, Victorian and South Australian parliaments decided to send naval contingents to China to participate in the suppression of the Boxer Rebellion. In Victoria the relevant motion passed without opposition; there was not even a division in either house of parliament.

In New South Wales the motion to support the involvement passed by fifty-six votes to seven, although there was spirited opposition to the venture.

The arguments of the triumphant majority are worth considering at some length. The leader for the government was the attorney-general, the intellectual and prominent federalist Bernhard Ringrose Wise. Educated in England, he was both imperialist and federalist. He wrote the classic history of the federal movement, *The Making of the Australian Commonwealth, 1889–1900*, with the telling subtitle *A Stage in the Growth of the Empire*. Wise demanded that his colleagues support the Chinese venture because if they didn't the international community would conclude that the colonies were regretting their involvement in South Africa. And by that commitment they had shown to the world that Britain could draw military strength from greater Britain. The appearance of the colonial forces in China would be noted by the other great powers represented in the international force. And China was even more important to Australia than South Africa. As a result, 'the highest obligation' was imposed on the country by its geographical position and it was because

> we are the outlying frontier of the white race upon this continent of yellow barbarism that the particular duty is cast upon us of doing all we can do to stem the awful danger that is now before, not only this country, but the whole white population of the world.[22]

Wise's ministerial colleague EW O'Sullivan declared that it was idle for men to say that the colonists should only organise to defend themselves. They could not do that because the only 'safety for our race lies in a strong unity'. The unification of Germany and Italy indicated that the 'Anglo-Saxon race' must take the same step and if it wasn't achieved,

> the nation to which we belong will retrograde into a second rate or third rate power. There is only one security against a danger of that kind, and it is – unification, harmony of action, and a determination to assert ourselves by all the means at our hand, to maintain the integrity of our race.[23]

The decision of the three colonial governments to send their naval forces to China was an easy one because of the extraordinary response, a few months before, of people all over Australia to news of the relief of the besieged British garrisons in Kimberley, Ladysmith and Mafeking. This was no doubt vividly remembered by deeply reassured politicians. The empire was at the height of its popularity. The imperial loyalists shared its lustre.

The three towns had been besieged by the Boer forces in the first weeks of the war, and early attempts to turn the tide were defeated in humiliating circumstances. Ladysmith was held hostage for 118 days, Kimberley for 124 and Mafeking for 217. Their fate was world news and symbolic of Britain's deep military humiliation. The empire was being held hostage by a citizen army of farmers. The suffering of the towns' residents, real and imagined, was reported across the empire. It was literally high drama. Tension intensified as long as the sieges persisted. The relief of the towns between the middle of February and the middle of May was a denouement of emotional intensity. News of the British victories was carried telegraphically into every corner of the continent. Spontaneous celebration broke out everywhere. News of the relief of Kimberley was received in the South Australian countryside by telegram from Adelaide early on a Saturday morning. At Victor Harbor 'the news spread rapidly, and in a brief space of time every flag was flying in the town'. When the first train arrived from Adelaide there was a rush to obtain copies of the *Advertiser*. In Eudunda, the flags flew and 'expressions of joy were heard on every side'. There was enthusiasm, too, in Yorketown. The *Advertiser*'s local correspondent reported how the British ensigns 'were sent to the breeze' and 'the local brass band played the "Soldiers of the Queen" and other patriotic pieces'.[24]

Celebration was more vociferous and widespread when news of the relief of Ladysmith was received early on Saturday morning, 3 March. In Hobart, sleepers were woken by the firing of the harbourside guns and the ringing of church bells. Crowds gathered in the city streets carrying flags. Small groups coalesced and marched up and down 'carolling joyously all the way'. The *Mercury* reporter thought that 'each countenance bore the imprint of fine exultant thankfulness'. One dancing reveller was heard to shout: 'Man … this is the glory of war'.[25] In Melbourne the bells rang and salutes boomed. Public feeling found its 'strongest expression' at the Stock Exchange. Members turned their backs on business and 'gave themselves up to enthusiastic demonstrations of patriotism'. Patriotic songs were sung with 'wild enthusiasm'. The 'members then formed into a procession and, carrying miniature Union Jacks', paraded up Collins Street. Late in the afternoon they were at it again. Headed by a brass band, they marched along Collins Street, sang the national anthem and 'indulged in hearty cheering'.[26] In Queensland, great enthusiasm prevailed in the country districts. Bonfires and torchlight processions illuminated tropical nights. Brisbane was bedecked with flags and red, white and blue bunting. The church bells rang and brass bands marched back and forth. The government declared a holiday on the following Monday for all public schools.

But the carnivals of celebration for Kimberley and Ladysmith were completely eclipsed by the colonial response to the relief of Mafeking, news of which was received in Australia at midday on Saturday, 19 May. Crowds exulted in their Britishness. It was 'a sign of deliverance and military triumph'.[27] The Hobart *Mercury* reported that from the sound of the first guns the whole town shook itself from ordinary cares and responsibilities 'and decided that it was a very good time to be alive with a British foot on British earth'.[28] The *Sydney Morning Herald* believed that revellers were 'proud to be classed as citizens of the same Empire as Mafeking's defenders'.[29] Reporters who mingled with the crowds were struck by the effect of the proceedings on ordinary people. In Hobart 'grave men of business, elders of repute in various seemly circles', lost their accustomed dignity of demeanour and 'deported themselves like street-boys'. 'Constitutionally moody and reserved' men were transformed. They became 'brisk as bees and open as the sunlight'.[30] The *Sydney Morning Herald* reported similarly, observing that 'All men were friends, ready to foregather, hop, skip, and sing any of the numerous national and patriotic themes which any precentor in the throng might choose for them. Even ladies allowed themselves to join in a more dignified way in the strangely moving access of enthusiasm'. Sydney was alive until late in the night. Rockets lit up the sky, and around the harbour red, blue and green fires could be seen. The ferries were draped with red, white and blue bunting. 'Roaring companies of men and boys', some of them four or six deep, pushed up and down King and George streets 'singing the same national songs that had been most in favour in the morning, sometimes three or four different ones together'.[31]

On the following Tuesday morning, Sydney's revellers were able to read in the *Herald* the details of how their country cousins had celebrated the relief of Mafeking. Reports had come in from ninety-three towns and villages. Mayors sent telegrams to congratulate the British military leaders and especially to Colonel Robert Baden-Powell, the commander in Mafeking and man of the hour. Flags and bunting were ubiquitous. The local brass bands had never been so busy. They led marches of detachments of volunteer soldiers, fire brigades and dignitaries. Dark rural nights came alive with torchlight processions, fireworks and bonfires. On the Sunday the churches were full to hear patriotic sermons. Hymns were mixed with songs of empire. The Union Jack was draped over pulpits. Services began and finished with the singing of the national anthem. Mars the god of war nestled comfortably with Christ the king of peace. At Glen Innes the children were given bags of locally made lollies engraved with the word 'Mafeking'. All reports described the excitement and joy expressed in their town and the enthusiasm for empire.[32]

There was certainly greater variety of opinion about the war almost everywhere than was suggested in the reports of celebration, but it must have been difficult in small towns to come out against the conflict. Dissent was an uncomfortable and even a dangerous stance to take in close-knit communities. There was a fight about the war outside a bar in Charters Towers and a man was shot. It was easier in the cities, where like-minded people could be found. But even there the great outburst of imperial loyalty must have been a dispiriting experience. The fact that the turn of events bore out many of the radicals' prophesies was no doubt some comfort, but there was no escaping the dramatic change that had taken place in Australian public life after the outbreak of the South African war.

8

The critics of the war

It was easier to express dissident opinions about the empire and the war in the colonial parliaments – and, after 1901, in the federal House of Representatives and the Senate – than in other public places. Judging from the reports of speeches, unpopular views were listened to with reasonable decorum, apart from occasional interjections. It no doubt also helped that in most of the parliaments, small groups of like-minded critics of majority opinion helped strengthen resolve and provide protection from that greatest handicap of dissident minorities – the sense of complete isolation and the wounding imputation of pointless eccentricity.

The dissenters shared common ground right across Australia; their opinions and speeches could have been interchangeable. And this happened without any apparent sharing of views or pooling of opinions. It is unlikely that parliamentarians knew much about what was happening in the other legislatures. If they actually read speeches made in the other colonies, it could only be much later, when official parliamentary debates were exchanged and lodged in the libraries. The major metropolitan newspapers reported intercolonial political events but rarely gave accounts of parliamentary debates. Australian politicians probably heard more about dissident opinion in Britain than in the sister parliaments. There was no doubt reassurance when it became apparent that some of Britain's most prominent and distinguished liberal politicians and intellectuals opposed the war. But the critical theme that ran through debates about the Boer War was almost entirely homegrown, relating more to local history than to the clash of opinion on the other side of the world. Considered in isolation, the small groups of dissenters could be disregarded, but looked at nationally they clearly represented a significant tradition that continues to have resonance more than a hundred years later.

Not all critics of the war could be thought of as radical nationalists, but they were certainly men whose focus was centred on Australia and who questioned the need for overseas involvement. In the debate in New South Wales on the Boxer Rebellion contingent, George Reid argued that 'the Australian military spirit is not for foreign service'. It was for the defence of the country. And that alone was a serious matter: 'With our enormous territory, as large as the United States, and our sparse population settled upon that vast surface, if we equip land forces sufficient for the defence of this great continent, we do all the empire can expect us to do'.[1]

In South Australia, during the Boer War debates, John Darling followed the same line of argument, feeling strongly that it was imprudent for the people of Australia to join in a quarrel outside the colonies. The local defence forces were for national defence and not for training men to be sent to fight in other parts of the world.[2] The distance between Australia and South Africa featured prominently in oppositional argument. The first proposition was that Australians were being sent to fight with and kill men they knew little about who could never present a threat to the Australian homeland. In Brisbane, WH Browne, the member for Croydon, thundered that

> to start unasked, uncalled for, and offer to send a lot of our young men out to train them up as into a quarrel we had no hand or part in, and which they know nothing about is the thing which should be deprecated by every member of this House.[3]

His colleague Henry Turley, from South Brisbane, savaged the government for forcing the colony into a fight they knew nothing about. Queensland should not be compelled to get into a quarrel which was not ours, which 'we had nothing whatever to do in bringing about' and which we should have 'nothing whatever to do in settling'.[4] In Perth, FC Vosper from the goldfields declared that he was totally out of sympathy with the idea of any of the colonies 'joining in a war-like policy against a small people, concerning whose grievances or troubles we know nothing'.[5] There was also anxiety about what was seen as nascent and unwelcome militarism. William Kidston, the member for Rockhampton, believed that the action of the government would turn members of the volunteer forces into soldiers, 'men who at a moment's notice' could be 'sent anywhere all over the world to fight in a quarrel they know nothing about'.[6] In Adelaide, WA Robinson asked: 'Why should our men without knowing anything about the struggle ... be expected to rush in and butcher those with whom they have no quarrel and whom they know nothing about?'[7]

As an alternative to war, the critics argued that the real business of the colonies was the development of the continent, a task that required all the capital and all the energies of the people. The struggle with nature was the truly authentic role of the country's young men, not the pursuit of imperial glory. William Sawers, the member for Tamworth, believed that New South Wales had 'far better and more important work to do than the encouragement of this military spirit'. The colony had 'the work of opening up and improving a vast virgin territory'.[8] George Reid declared that Australians did 'not want to be looked upon as a military people' who were 'ready to send their contingents forth to do battle in any part of the globe'. It was 'time to put the heel upon that contemptible way of trying to advertise this country by a readiness to offer up our men upon any shrine of blood that offers itself'.[9] In Melbourne, John Murray condemned 'the cultivation of a warlike spirit' in the colony. 'We are', he said, 'essentially a commercial people, and we should never be delighted to fight' unless it was 'in defence of our own country'.[10] His colleague WA Watt said much the same thing, arguing that 'the genius of the Australian people has hitherto been pacific', although the time could come when it might be necessary to fight for the 'rights and privileges, which our fathers have won for us in this country'.[11] In the same debate, JW McCay warned that the South African venture would, without doubt, 'encourage the spirit of militarism in this colony', warning darkly, 'if we taste blood, we shall probably want to taste it again' and would be 'more liable to engage in future military operations'.[12] In Adelaide, Thomas Price warned that Australia was entering into Federation 'with the intention of creating a military spirit', which would be the first step towards 'tarnishing [Australians'] good name as makers and builders of a nation'. The federal movement would be transformed into a military movement.[13] In Brisbane, WH Browne was strenuously opposed to raising 'a military caste' in the colony.[14]

Several politicians recommended what today we would call a humanitarian option, Dr William Moloney arguing in the Victorian parliament, 'if we are to give any help at all from this country, we should give it in a manner consistent with the interests of humanity, and send a ship laden with provisions to the assistance of the women and children who have been made hungry by this wretched business'.[15]

Imperialists in New South Wales were proud to claim the Sudan contingent as the forerunner of the united involvement in South Africa. During the celebrations that marked the departure of the first contingent from Sydney, the statue of William Dalley was draped in patriotic bunting, while on 3 March 1900 a salute of twenty-one guns was fired in commemoration of the anniversary of the earlier departure. But in the other colonies, where the South African venture was unprecedented, the critics saw it as a radical departure from all previous experience. Colonial policy towards the outside world had been upturned. The matters in contention were illustrated in an exchange in the Queensland parliament. JC Stewart accused the premier of altering the foreign policy of the colony. The Minister for Railways, John Murray, interjected: 'We have no foreign policy here'. To which Stewart replied: 'This colony and Australia generally has had a foreign policy', which hitherto had been one 'of non-interference in matters outside the colony'. With that the treasurer, Robert Philp, called out: 'You are quite wrong'. Stewart retorted that the colony's foreign policy had been one of 'absolute non-interference in the quarrels of the Empire'.[16] Returning to the same theme, William Kidston declared that the government had brought about 'a radical change in the foreign policy of Queensland'. Are we to understand, he asked,

> that this is the beginning of a new time in relation to the Imperial Government, whether we are to understand that every time after this when Great Britain is engaged in a war anywhere throughout the whole world, that a contingent of armed men from Queensland will be sent to take part in that war … If the offering of this contingent is so necessary now to show the loyalty of Queensland, would it not be just as necessary to show this loyalty in the event of

> another war? ... If the next Premier does not do this, then Queensland will be blamed for being disloyal. It seems to me that to admit that the action that has been taken is right, opens the flood-gates very wide indeed ...

Kidston finished with a flourish, asking if the premier had 'considered the far-reaching consequences of this proposed action'.[17]

His sentiments and concerns were echoed in every colonial parliament. Time and again critics pointed to the fact that precedents were being established, the significance of which would reverberate across the years. The line of common argument was clear. With its vast empire, Britain would continue to be involved in war both large and small. History pointed emphatically in that direction. In the past, the Australian colonies had not been involved, apart from the anomalous and contentious New South Wales intervention in the Sudan. The collective commitment to South Africa was another matter altogether. In 1899 there seemed to be no pressing necessity for the involvement of Australian troops – and the war was controversial. In many parts of the world it was seen as an aggressive and illegitimate attack by a vast empire on two small independent republics. If intervention was effected then and there, was there any possibility that the future Federation could escape ongoing involvement? There would be no end to it. Clearly the imperial government would expect nothing less, and indeed would take it for granted that Australians would henceforth contribute to future conflict and make its war plans accordingly. How could Australia avoid this predetermined fate?

The arguments in 1900 in favour of involvement in the repression of the Boxer Rebellion bore out these forebodings. The contention was that a refusal to become engaged would suggest a significant change of policy and a political rebuff to the empire. The critics' retort was that it was much easier to get into a war than to avoid one. In the New South Wales parliament, James Ashton observed that the involvement in China was 'practically to commit Australia for all time to the sending of troops into every international complication that may arise'.[18] And there was no way of knowing how long an engagement would last and what future demands would follow the initial one. As JC Stewart observed in the Queensland parliament during the Boer War debate, the premier had come forward and asked for £32 000,

> but any person who has read the history of England must know that when Great Britain engages in a war, something like a bottomless pit is opened up with regard to expense. You may know the beginning, but you do not know how or where or when it will end.[19]

Of the many colonial politicians who spoke out against the rush to war, the most significant was HB Higgins, both because of his future importance as federal minister, High Court judge and arbitration commissioner, and because of the power and cogency of his case against war in both the Victorian and Australian parliaments. Higgins was

British-born and expressed his continuing affection for what he referred to as the mother country, but he had a clear idea of how his adopted country should develop. 'The ideal of Australia', he declared, 'is peace; the peaceful development of our great resources and the peaceful employment of our people'.[20] The involvement in South Africa was both immoral and unnecessary. 'Look at the shabbiness of it all', he later said, challenging his colleagues. What was wanted was 'men to develop Australia; we do not want men to desolate South Africa. We want men who will build homes in Australia, not men who will burn homes in South Africa'.[21]

Perhaps more than any other Australian politician, Higgins was concerned about the morality of war. He was exercised by the fact that the colonies had plunged into a war they knew little about. He observed at the beginning that his Victorian colleagues took the view, common also in the other colonies, that they should not 'inquire too closely into the justice of the quarrel. That', he cried,

> is what I object to. I say that we have no right whatever to enter into any war … unless we do enter into the justice of it. It seems to me to shock all conscience for us to venture to go into a war with a light heart, and without inquiring closely into the justice of it.[22]

When, in January 1902, the Australian parliament debated the commitment of a federal force to the war, Higgins attacked Prime Minister Barton because he had 'not disclosed to the House any grounds upon which the soldiers of Australia ought to be sent to kill the Boer farmers'.

It was, he observed, a 'very extreme step' that the Prime Minister should invite Australian men 'to try to kill men … with whom they have had no relations, direct or indirect'.[23] The flagrant error that had been committed by the colonies before Federation was now being committed by the new Commonwealth. He confessed that he had 'hoped better things of Australia as a whole'.[24] In a lecture delivered in July 1902, entitled 'The duties of patriotism', he took careful aim at the saying 'Our country, right or wrong', which he had heard Prime Minister Barton mouth in the parliament. It was, he said, a fallacy that was 'at the root of that narrow patriotism' which excluded 'unpleasant truths' and which rendered 'possible the continuance of that extraordinary anomaly – war between two bodies of civilised people, who have never met or dealt with one another, but who are merely told that the others are enemies'.[25]

Higgins developed his ideas further in an article published at about the same time as when, in January 1902, he took a lonely stand against war in the federal parliament. He posed the question of whether militarism was corrupting the new nation and undermining the colonial commitment to equality. He observed that some of the finest of the nation's youth had been seduced by the lure of imperial loyalty 'to seek distinction in the battlefield in a distant country'. The local newspapers and public men as well had insisted that it was a worthy aim for young Australians to fight side by side with imperial troops, 'whatever might be the cause of the war'. What did Australia gain by mixing in the world's quarrels, 'from which the remoteness of our island continent happily exempts us'? The true ideals of the country were peace and internal development. But beyond his opposition to the South African war, he was concerned about a pervasive growth of militarism, as we have seen above.[26]

By 1902 there was little parliamentary opposition to the war. Few of the men who spoke out about the venture in the colonial parliaments in 1899 transferred to the federal sphere, where henceforward matters of war, peace and external relations were determined. It may be that many politicians who were initially opposed to the war bent before the drift of imperial loyalty. Higgins himself was defeated in the Victorian election in 1900, largely as a result of his dissident stance. AI Clark agreed with him, but a seat on the Supreme Court bench in Tasmania silenced him. His son Carrel explained that the outbreak of the Boer War found his father, in his private capacity, 'a firm and sincere denouncer of Chamberlain's action towards the Boer Republic'. He held that Britain had no right – moral or legal – to coerce the Transvaal. It was the manifestation of 'that most hateful, to him, of all policies – an aggressive and blustering imperialism'.[27] The feminist leader Rose Scott was equally incensed by Australia's involvement in the war, and its impact on the mothers and wives of the soldiers, who had

> no power to say whether or not, an evil and barbaric war shall mow down their sons upon the hills and plains of a distant land. When the contingent went away, no more pathetic sight could be seen than men, women and little children rushing about to see them

> off. 'Will they all get killed?' cried a poor little boy to his father. Let us ask, how many Boer fathers, brothers, sons and husbands will they kill? But let those who make quarrels be the only men to fight and let no nation be called worthy … who resorts to physical force instead of moral suasion.[28]

In her journal *The Dawn*, Louisa Lawson linked the inauguration of the Federation with the proclamation of a great and bloody war, and as a result 'hot drops of this dark and bloody baptism burnt into the hearts of the mothers of Australia', who were expected to 'bid adieu perhaps for ever to the sons they loved so well'. She penned a poignant account of 'these unhappy mothers half stunned and altogether desolate' at the edge of the ocean as the troop ship slipped from sight. 'God comfort them', she prayed, 'these mothers of men, for no matter how great the victories gained or battles won, no atom of honour or glory will fall to them in recognition of all they have suffered or sacrificed to their country's cause. *They are women*'.[29]

The most prominent non-parliamentary opponent of the war was George Arnold Wood, the Challis professor of history at Sydney University, who engaged in a public debate in local newspapers and wrote to the *Manchester Guardian*, activities that provoked vehement opposition and led to demands for his dismissal. Wood endeavoured to explain to his Sydney readers the nature and extent of opposition to the war in Britain. He was convinced of the immorality of British policy, and on the eve of the conflict expressed his hope that New South Wales would refuse to 'make itself an accomplice in this war of cowardly revenge and ignoble greed'.[30] He was particularly incensed by the much-repeated phrase 'Our country, right or wrong', with its implication that the justice or injustice of the war was a matter of no importance.[31] His outrage deepened towards the end of the war, when news emerged of the concentration camps in which the British imprisoned civilians and of fire and pillage on the veldt (see chapter 9). It was behaviour that was bringing 'everlasting infamy upon the English name'.[32]

Wood's lonely crusade was discussed by Alfred Deakin in one of his regular contributions to the London *Morning Post*. It was dismissive to the point of ridicule. Wood, Deakin insisted, was a member of a 'knot of sympathisers with Mr Kruger' who could not obtain a hearing for, much less assent to, their doctrines in New South Wales. They had been unable to carry a single public meeting in Sydney or out of it, to obtain the countenance of a single public man or journal of the first or second rank. Apart from Deakin's partisan invective, the most interesting aspect of his exegesis was that Wood's ideas were un-Australian. They were, he insisted, 'not an Australian growth'. The professor, Deakin charged, had brought them with him from Britain and he would take them away again. He was as immersed in the doctrines of the Manchester School as he had been when he left Britain ten years before, and was unable to understand or appreciate what Deakin called the 'Imperial instinct of his race'.[33] The assessment is rich in its implications. Deakin had pointed to a significant feature of colonial liberalism. It had sloughed off the traditions of what he called the Manchester School, by which he meant that central thread of British liberalism associated with Cobden, Bright and Gladstone. It had become unpopular among many colonists because of its assumed indifference to the colonies. By 1900 it was seen to be old-fashioned and no longer relevant, particularly in the go-ahead white dominions. But it cut Australian political life off from one of the most important intellectual sources of liberalism, one that has remained far more relevant to the contemporary world than Deakin's worship of blood, race and the imperial instinct.

Other implications can be readily found. Deakin's proposition suggests that there had been a narrowing down of Australian political life, a drift to conformity. The public and political reaction to the Boer War was symptomatic. There was much greater opposition in Britain itself than in Australia. The British Liberal Party was deeply divided on the issue. Up to a third of members of the House of Commons were known as pro-Boer. Irish and Welsh members made up part of this anti-war faction. But underlying the dissent was the bedrock of Gladstonian liberalism, with its scepticism about war, a preference for mediation, hostility to military expenditure, and a moral concern for the consequences of war for both individuals and society alike. There was, too, a residue of Cobden and Bright's anguish for the victims of war among both allies and enemies. Significant numbers of British politicians had an inherited immunity to the seductive appeal of imperialism and jingoism.

The New South Wales politician John Haynes observed with considerable acuity what was happening to Australian politics. He noted the greater spirit of dissent in the Commons where, he observed, you would never hear anyone dare say that because a man might disagree with the proposal for war, he was consequently a traitor. It was different in Australia. 'Manful independence' had been swamped in a tide of conformity. 'We have come step by step to this condition of affairs', he observed,

> that the leading men in our public life are automatons; they are not independent men when it comes to expressing public opinion, or taking action with regard to any matter which involves war. One of the most important things which has come out of this debate is the unquestionable evidence of the fact that during the last ten years, and particularly during the last four or five years, there has been, notwithstanding their personal and ostensible political differences, a drifting of a certain class of politicians towards one centre.

He explained that both liberal and conservative members of the Legislative Assembly were at one in 'all matters bearing upon what I might call soldier operations'. There was instant cooperation between them and a common instinct operating in their minds. It was, he concluded, an 'extraordinary state of things'.[34]

The difference between Britain and Australia showed up most strikingly in the response to the manner in which the imperial forces conducted the latter stages of the war, including the scorched-earth policy on the veldt and the incarceration of civilians in concentration camps with disastrous results. The sensational reports of British welfare campaigner Emily Hobhouse about the scandalous conditions in the concentration camps (see chapter 9) had a direct impact on British attitudes, leading to a decisive shift in liberal opinion. After a meeting with Hobhouse, the Liberal leader, Henry Campbell-Bannerman, moved decisively towards the pro-Boers, denouncing the tactics being used as 'methods of barbarism'. The situation in the camps was fully debated in the Commons in June 1901. David Lloyd George mounted a detailed and savage attack on the way the war was being conducted. The government carried the day, but 134 members voted against it. There was also a strong group of critics of the war outside the parliament, including some of the most prominent intellectuals and artists in the country.

Nothing comparable occurred in Australia. There appeared to be an absence of moral concern about the war itself or about the methods of barbarism. There was a clear reluctance to accept any responsibility for what was happening out on the veldt. There was no discussion in the Australian parliament about the concentration camps. The only serious consideration of the war came in a debate in January 1902, which dealt with the dispatch of an Australian contingent, as opposed to a colonial one, to the war. But members did address the mounting chorus of criticism of British tactics in both Britain itself and in Europe and America. In the House of Representatives the government had overwhelming support. The vote to send the new contingent was forty-five to five. With that, Prime Minister Barton announced: 'I think that both sides of the House will now heartily join in giving three cheers for King and Empire'. The Hansard recorded that 'members then rose in their places and cheered'.[35]

During the debate there were references to the conduct of the war. Barton acknowledged that Australian troops were serving under British generals. But that, in itself, was reassuring because the British officers could be trusted and were bound to subscribe to the articles of war. George Reid insisted that all the disreputable reports were 'wholesale fabrications', but they had to be repudiated because 'the Empire must be supported; the character of our race must be vindicated'. It was obvious the stories of barbarism were false because the historical record showed that British soldiers and sailors had been conspicuous for their 'tenderness and humanity' once the battle was over. The Labor Party members outdid their political opponents in their deference to the empire. JC Watson believed that 'never in the history of nations has a war been conducted with a greater regard for humanity than the Boer war'.[36] In the Senate, GF Pearce asserted that this had been 'the most humane war' the world had ever seen. Senator Sir John Downer believed the Boers were happy that their women and children were in kind British hands. The motion supporting the dispatch of the federal contingent passed on the voices. There was no report of cheers for King and empire.[37]

Alfred Deakin was playing to his British audience when he dismissed the opponents of the war, claiming they had no support in either the first- or second-rank journals. In fact, there was a good deal of criticism in a range of papers, and nowhere more significant than in the Sydney *Bulletin*, which had a wide intercolonial readership. It opened its campaign on the eve of the war with inimitable verve. Some of us, wrote Henry Lawson, are willing – 'wilfully, blindly, eager, mad! – to cross the sea and shoot men whom we never saw and whose quarrel we do not and cannot understand'. The Sudan campaign was bad enough, a blot on 'our history for ever'. 'I tell you', he confided, that the thing we are going to do about the Transvaal 'is ten times more shameful'.[38] A correspondent, 'R.S.', contributed a scurrilous verse, 'The Jingo Parson's Curse', which ran:

> *Now that war is in the air, e'en the parson in his lair*
> *Is seized with wild desirings for the sight of spurting*
> *blood.*
> *And he pitches it so strong to his sanctimonious throng*
> *That they almost hear in fancy bodies falling with a*
> *thud.*
> *Let me see my neighbour's blood*
> *Spouting out in crimson flood.*[39]

In an early editorial, JF Archibald damned the leading politicians for their readiness to become involved in Britain's wars without asking any questions about their justice or injustice. But even if the war were a just one, the country would have no excuse for involvement. The first duty of Australians was to Australia:

> To mindlessly waste men and money in foreign war, and in about the worst possible cause, is nothing less than a national crime; and the Militia officers and

> politicians who committed Australia to war would be promptly impeached for treason in any country where existed an honest and intelligent public spirit. The more you reflect on it, the more unthinkable it is that Australia should send Australians to shoot and be shot by Boers in South Africa with whom we have no quarrel. Why, when men and money are so badly needed here to develop Australia, should we pile up debts for our children to pay, or risk the lives of men who should be rearing Australian families? *Here*, in Australia – not in Africa or Britain.[40]

The radicals associated with the journal were confounded by the war's popularity, by the rush to recruit and by the hostility that confronted the critics, increasingly condemned as pro-Boers. Archibald addressed an editorial to the working men concerning 'these militant misguided men' who were clamouring to go to war. What were they thinking about, he asked, when they volunteered to 'abet the blood guilty schemes of a Tory government in its designs on a democratic republic …' It was to their eternal discredit that they went to war without first learning the facts about the conflict. In fact, Australians should admire the 'magnificent patriotism animating the Dutch burghers', who had left their farms and families to defend with their lives the integrity of their native land.[41]

The anguish of an Australian patriot in the midst of a popular imperial war was caught by a correspondent, 'C.M.G.', in January 1900. He found that even liberal-minded English-born friends were unable or unwilling to appreciate or understand his Australian point of view. Although his parents were English, he explained:

> Any sentiment of loyalty I possess is entirely Australian: my interest in England is nowise different from my interest in Germany, France or America. It is, in fact, purely literary, never personal; and because of this my critics call me traitor … I am called a hater of England because I do not sing 'Soldiers of the Queen' … Asseverations of my Australianism provoke incredulous contempt – what is there to take hold of in this pitiful Australia, without history, age or accomplishment? … From inherited patriotism in young Australians spring blood-lusting contingents to battle not for Australia in Australia, but for England in Africa.[42]

A tone of bitterness crept into the pages of *The Bulletin* as the war progressed, with references to 'the ingratitude of the people to those who strive to show them the right path'.[43] There was insufficient appreciation of the fact that the war 'marked a crisis in Australian public life'. But the true issue did not come before the Australian people. Their leaders deceived them, newspapers deceived them,

> and instead of declaring for liberty, throwing in the scale the weight of influence of free colonies on behalf of Freedom and Right, they declared for the bloody suppression of claims for which their own struggles should have taught them full sympathy. *That* was the great false step, from which we have marched on to

> militarism, suppression of free speech, and revival of the royal 'divine right' fetish, the general growth of Conservative tyranny ... It was a sinister mistake, the adoption of a jingo policy by Australia.[44]

In the same issue a contributor submitted a piece of verse entitled 'The Lost Ideal', which read in part:

> *His sacred trust we tread in the dust at the beat of a drum!*
> *We flaunt our rags under fluttering flags when the soldiers come;*
> *We prattle the story of bloodshed and 'glory' in alley and slum.*
> *The buttons and braid of the bloody trade are ours today*
> *The tools of Labor are rifle and sabre, its motto 'To Slay'.*[45]

But *The Bulletin* was not alone. Other papers and magazines took up the cause, including the radical Melbourne journal *Tocsin*, the labour paper *The Clipper* in Hobart and *The Worker* in Brisbane, the official journal of the Federated Workers of Queensland. Writers in *Tocsin* expressed an abiding moral concern about popular support for the war arising from 'a blind belief in our own nationality'.[46] As a result, the working men of the country yelled 'hurrah' and hardly a man or woman 'feels the stain of blood upon the national conscience'. The brand of murderer sat 'very lightly on the collective mass'.[47] The pity was that Australians were overcome by the unreasoning hysteria 'of a people drunk with a sentiment and excited by the delusion that they are playing a creditable part in the history of the world'.[48] The Victorian decision to send a naval contingent to China evoked intensified anguish about 'the artificially fostered madness' that had clouded the public mind overcome by 'the un-Australian imperialism'. The future looked bleak:

> Is this country to be under the stigma of having a band of homicides at work in every spot on the globe where murder is going on? The time was when we took pride in our Australia as a land of peace. Shall it depart from us for ever to be the British Imperialist Jingo Cliques Australia, and kennel of the foremost dogs of war? Have we sunk so low?[49]

A common theme in much of the anti-war literature echoed HB Higgins' concerns, one writer regretting the growing 'spirit of militarism which had swept like a hurricane over the land'.[50] The editor of *Tocsin* appealed to the country's democratic spirit, 'hidden surely some where yet in Australian's hearts', to come out of its hiding place and save Australia from 'impending militaristic … catastrophe'.[51] Militarism was, the radicals declared, the antithesis of democracy: 'Militarism implies unquestioned authority, such authority implies caprice, caprice implies inequality, injustice, ranks of the people, and childish restrictions on tongue, manner and pen … We have voluntarily put our fingers on to a militaristic battery from which we shall be unable to draw them when we wish …'[52]

Brisbane's *Worker* was the most consistent opponent of the war and never let its hostility flag in the face of popular enthusiasm. The Queensland labour movement generally maintained a more consistently unbending stance than the fraternal parties in the other states. The *Worker*'s emphasis was on the influence of the capitalist companies on the Rand goldfields, with a significant element of anti-Semitism aimed at the Jewish mine owners. The ability of capitalism to exploit popular sentiment was the reason for enthusiasm for the war, because they 'rally the people – the simple gullible people who are always willing to be led – with sentimental cries'. The editor hoped that the workers, while still preserving their affection for the old country, 'give over whooping and shouting for the Imperial capitalist class' and discontinue helping them to carry out their 'sentiment-gilded schemes'.[53] A short time before the end of the war, a correspondent under the pen-name, 'The Philistine' contributed an article entitled 'What war is', which opened with a long quotation from John Bright's passionate appeal to the community on the eve of the Crimean War and then followed up with its own distinctive denunciation of unnecessary wars:

> Knowing what war is, and how it debases the best of peoples, and what hideous atrocities are perpetrated and fostered under its cloak, the statesman who leaves a single stone unturned for peace before plunging the nation into war is a criminal of blacker dye than any of which the records of our gaols can tell.[54]

The radical papers appealed to a small audience and almost certainly lost circulation during the course of the conflict. But they remind us that there was much more to say about the war than appeared in the major newspapers, full of highly partisan stories from London and South Africa. Australians were shielded from much of the analysis that appeared in other parts of the world. That highly partial account has continued to influence the way modern Australia thinks about the war that ushered in both the 20th century and Federation.

9

Involvement in an infamous war

The imperial cause triumphed in Australia between 1899 and 1902. There were critics of the war, and interest among the public probably flagged in the final months of the conflict, but the politicians who took Australia to war did not suffer any serious consequences from their commitment to the British cause. When the soldiers returned they were treated as heroes in their home suburbs, towns and districts. Monuments were commissioned all over the continent, and many of them remain in place. The minority tradition that bracketed nationalism, republicanism and international neutrality was overwhelmed by imperial loyalty, the monarchy and a sudden penchant for war. Some of the war's opponents were aware of the provenance of their ideas, the *Tocsin* quoting passages from John Dunmore Lang. But the most important legacy of the dissident tradition was that it had continuing cogency, while the competing imperial cause rested on what proved extremely insecure foundations. The argument of Lang and many subsequent Australians that the empire was a source of danger rather than a sanctuary was fully vindicated. Close proximity to a great imperial power was perilous, and predetermined involvement in war. In this way the Boer War was both paradigmatic and prophetic of future wars. The dissidents' belief that Australia's size, isolation and surrounding seas were strategic assets proved to be more relevant than the alternative idea that the continent was irremediably vulnerable, requiring the protection of a great and powerful friend.

Even more directly relevant was the reality that imperial power and grandeur were ephemeral. So much store was invested in the belief of an enduring empire. So much endeavour, intellectual, emotional and political, had been premised on continuity. But the children born in the year of Federation lived to see the empire shrink into geopolitical irrelevance. Dependence on the ailing empire proved a deeply flawed strategy. Deference to its leaders produced little of enduring value but made Australia's leaders vulnerable to manipulation. The faith of the imperialists was understandable – the empire of the early 20th century was imposing – but the signs of decline were already showing in 1901.

The truth was that in the early years of the 20th century, Britain needed Australia more than the new

Federation needed the old empire. This was better understood in London than in Melbourne. CP Lucas, one of the ablest members of the Colonial Office, wrote in 1912 that it was essential for Britain to keep the dominions with her if she was to 'hold her own as a nation'. In fact, he observed:

> it is probably true to say, though it may not be generally admitted, that as each succeeding year adds conspicuously to the population of the young peoples of the world, whether inside or outside the British Empire, the value of the Dominions increases in much greater proportion than the value of England to the Dominions, because each year each Dominion comes nearer to the time when it can defend itself, and each year England, without the Dominions, tends to be more outdistanced in population and home resources by some of her foreign competitors.[1]

One of the most powerful bulwarks of imperial loyalty was the expectation that Britain would ultimately guarantee Australia's security, but intimations of weakness were apparent from 1870, when Britain conceded it could not garrison the empire. And by 1900 the Admiralty had concluded it was unable to compete with the United States in the western hemisphere or with Japan in north-eastern Asia. But imperial sentiment always clouded calculation. To doubt the empire's durability was seen to be disloyal. To apply the normal calculation of profit and loss was thought to be inappropriate when dealing with kin.

Ultimately, colonial deference served British interests

rather than the interests of the dominions, whose leaders were characteristically far too trusting. They believed in family loyalty more strongly than did the British leadership. As far back as the 1860s, CW Dilke had cast doubt on the likelihood of Britain defending Australia, writing:

> As for our so-called defence of the colonies, in war-time we defend ourselves; we defend the colonies only during peace. In war-time they are ever left to shift for themselves, and they would undoubtedly be better fit to do so were they in the habit of maintaining their military establishments in time of peace.[2]

Another illusion of the time was the belief in the conceptual and political potency of race. There was a widespread belief that the 'British race' had innate qualities that gave its members the capacity to govern and rule over less favoured peoples. Racial theory also created the illusion that blood determined strategic cohesion on the one hand and international hostility on the other. Biology drew Australians towards Britain and worked in the opposite way with China and Japan, which many Australians believed were predestined to become enemies. Racial solidarity and family loyalty would, it was widely believed, ensure that Britain would come to Australia's defence at any future time of crisis. But there was more to it than that. In a debate in the federal parliament in 1904, Thomas Ewing insisted that the country had no future 'except as part of the Empire … under the British flag'. Given the proximity of China and Japan, 'it would be impossible for Australia to exist as a separate nation for any great period'. Every one of his colleagues, he declared, knew that the country would be 'swallowed at one gulph [sic] by these nations if she did not form part of the Empire'. Permanent occupation of the continent by a 'white race' was only possible 'under the flag of Great Britain and in no other way'.[3] Such views were widely shared.

There had been much popular hostility towards Britain in both Europe and North America during the war in South Africa. Goldwin Smith declared in March 1900 that Britain had 'drawn upon herself the execration of mankind'.[4] International public opinion was firmly on the side of the Transvaal and the Orange Free State.[5] The Boer generals became popular figures for their defiant struggle against overwhelming odds. The vast difference in power and population between the combatants led to the common judgment that Britain was engaged in a war that was unjust, unnecessary and unfair. The involvement of Australia, New Zealand and Canada was not seen overseas, as people in the dominions supposed, as an indication of familial solidarity, but as both a symptom of British weakness and an even clearer enhancement of her reputation as a global bully. Internationally, 'anglophobia reached new heights'.[6] The determination to crush Boer resistance, to refuse to accept any outcome short of annexation, confirmed in many minds the conviction that the British were the high priests of hypocrisy, who talked of how their benign rule brought peace to the world while fighting endless wars against enemies who had no hope of resisting them. One saving grace was that many of the most effective critics of

British imperialism were themselves British – figures such as the liberal philosopher Leonard Hobhouse, brother of anti-war activist Emily, who asked in 1904: 'What, then, were the fruits of Imperialism?' Answering his own question he observed:

> Did it, for example, give us peace? On the contrary, the perplexed observer, looking vainly for the British peace which was to be, was confronted with an endless succession of frontier wars, some small, some great, but all ending with annexation of further territory. Under the reign of Imperialism the temple of Janus is never closed. Blood never ceases to run. The voice of the mourner is never hushed.[7]

Australia's imperial enthusiasm perplexed many outside observers. Why did the colonies want to be involved in a war so far away against another nation of white settlers who could never present any threat to the continent? Why wasn't there more concern about the way the British authorities had overridden the opinion of so many of the prominent leaders of the parliament in the Cape Colony? Why didn't more Australians identify with, or at least display sympathy for, the small besieged republics? And why did societies that made much of their spirit of frontier independence show so little of it when it came to the dictates of the Colonial Office? The American diplomatic historian PS Reinsch observed in 1901 that the colonial leaders had

> managed to satisfy their consciences, and the consciences of their people, by unanimous and wholesale indorsement of everything that the Colonial Secretary has done or has wished to do in South Africa. This may have saved them the trouble of thinking; it may have elicited a blessing from Downing Street; but whether it be true loyalty is doubtful.[8]

Perhaps even more pertinently, why did the colonies that were among the most democratic societies in the world behave with such deference to the British aristocratic ruling class? Why did Australian leaders side so decisively with a conservative British government and react with hostility to the Liberal Party then in opposition? And why did they appear to have a powerful taste for war and cling to every favourable comment about their military prowess? Why were they so susceptible to the flattery of any British observer? Were democracies inherently warlike? Were egalitarian societies more conformist than more hierarchical ones? The Boer War had overturned a common contemporary assumption that democracies would not be warlike. Hobhouse observed that after the enthusiastic participation of the dominions in the Boer War it 'must certainly rank among the shattered illusions'.[9]

The Australian opponents of the war were often aware of overseas criticism of British policies and tactics, and found some comfort in the fact. But such criticism could be more liability than asset. The empire loyalists were infuriated by overseas judgment and were confirmed in their belief that there was a global conspiracy against Britain, a belief that reinforced rather than weakened their commitment to the empire. For Australian dissidents to refer to foreign critics was regarded as a form of disloyalty inexcusable at a time when Britain was under stress. And Australian politicians proved remarkably adept at averting their eyes from any unwelcome information. News from the front was carefully crafted, and the Australian correspondents in South Africa knew the stories their readers wanted to hear.

But experience in South Africa challenged perceptions brought from Australia. The crudest anti-Boer propaganda fell away, to be replaced by grudging respect. Australians from the countryside came to realise that in many ways they had more in common with the Boers than with their British patrons. Another revelation was that there was much hostility towards the war in the Cape Colony, where it was seen as a disastrous civil conflict engineered by the British authorities and their English-born and English-speaking colonial allies. It came as a shock to Australians disembarking at Cape Town that there was none of the exuberant cheering that had accompanied their departure. Met with sullen silence, they quickly realised that by many South Africans they were not seen as saviours and liberators. Many of the most articulate leaders of Cape society found it hard to understand why the other dominions had become needlessly involved, compounding the disaster.

AB (Banjo) Paterson, who went to South Africa at the beginning of the conflict as a correspondent for major metropolitan newspapers, provided highly acceptable and entirely conventional copy emphasising the fighting qualities of the Australian forces. But he was forced to the realisation that many South Africans opposed both the war and the Australian involvement. He reported that it would surprise many of his readers to hear that in the Cape Colony there were more people against the war than for it. They were not necessarily Boer sympathisers but people who thought the war should never have been entered into. This confrontation with reality reached a high point when Paterson interviewed the celebrated South African writer Olive Schreiner, who said of the involvement of the dominion troops: 'I cannot understand it at all, why you come here light-heartedly to shoot down other colonists of whom you know nothing – it is terrible'. It was, she declared, 'a monstrous war' and she correctly saw that it would drag on and become even more disastrous, believing it would end up being 'a war of extermination'.[10]

Other equally prominent public figures in the English-speaking world were highly critical of the dominion involvement in South Africa and felt that it had been initiated with an irresponsible insouciance. JX Merriman, one of the most distinguished Cape politicians, expressed his feelings in letters to like-minded liberals in other parts of the empire, including Goldwin Smith in Canada, who was a prominent opponent of the war, and the leading British Liberal James Bryce. In a letter to Bryce in December 1899, Merriman expressed his anguish about the horrors of a civil war, explaining that there was not a family in the Cape that did not have friends and relatives fighting for the Boers. It was no wonder, he explained, that their feelings were intense and bitter. It made the involvement of the dominion forces both inexplicable and intolerable. He told Goldwin Smith that the other colonies were meddling in what should have been a domestic quarrel. The enlistment of colonial contingents was 'peculiarly odious'. The quarrel was not their quarrel and 'they simply come for excitement'.[11] The involvement of the self-governing dominions was also inexplicable because the British government had so blatantly overridden the authority of the Cape parliament, setting at odds principles of responsible government that had been embraced by the other dominions since the middle of the 19th century. Goldwin Smith wondered why the dominions were so keen to associate with Britain in a crusade to crush the independence of two small states. In the early months of the year he predicted that the Boers would inevitably be defeated, but they had 'put in a telling caveat against the assumption that the world is the property of a few great powers, and in favour of the community of nations'.[12]

Merriman received reports of atrocities committed by the Australians in the Northern Cape quite early in the war. They shot Africans and terrorised a local farming community while conducting what he called a marauding raid. 'These swashbucklers', he wrote, 'arrested inhabitants, drove off stock, and shot a few people without greatly caring who they were'. The victims were 'full of grievances against the Australians'.[13] There were many other reports of this kind, relating not just to enemy territory but to the Cape Colony as well. The Australians had a bad reputation for ill-treating Africans. One study of the war concluded that a substantial proportion of the assaults upon blacks in the army and upon Indian and Chinese civilians could be attributed to the colonial contingents, 'notably Australians'.[14] But the violence reported by Merriman was only a foretaste of what was to come in 1901 and 1902 as the Boers launched highly skilled guerrilla raids against the imperial army all over South Africa, including the Cape itself.

General HH Kitchener, the imperial commander, had two objectives. He wanted to bring the war to an end as quickly as possible, with the complete capitulation of the Boer forces, their acquiescence in the annexation of the two republics and their absorption into the empire. He initiated a fierce and relentless campaign against the whole Boer population. It had two main features. The army swept the veldt to remove the civilian population, principally women, children, old people and African servants. They were imprisoned in concentration camps. Farmhouses were burnt, their contents smashed or stolen, crops destroyed and farm animals killed. Troops were given licence to loot, smash and intimidate. The results were terrible and scandalised the world. In all, the British forces burnt more than 30 000 Boer farms and forty towns. They destroyed or stole millions of head of livestock.[15] They burnt crops, wrecked machinery and cut through dam walls.

But a greater horror unfolded in the concentration camps. They were hastily prepared tent cities, often on the open veldt, overcrowded, with limited fresh water and primitive sanitation. The food was inadequate and of poor quality. The death rate was catastrophic during the period when the army had control of the camps – 160 000 Boers were incarcerated, 28 000 died, more than 22 000 of them children. More than 100 000 Africans were placed in even more ramshackle camps, where at least 14 000 died, 80 per cent of them children.[16] The South African historian Bill Nasson drew attention to the disastrous impact of the war:

> Horrendously high mortality rates in British concentration camps, and the loss of perhaps as much as 20 per cent of the tiny Boer republican populations, meant that it represented a form of historical trauma for Afrikaner society, the depth of which imperial and other English-speaking historians have perhaps rarely fully recognized.[17]

South Africans who knew what was happening were deeply concerned that a terrible precedent had been established. Merriman remarked that that someday 'we may regret that we put these principles of warfare into vogue'.[18] When the Boer general Louis Botha came in from the field to discuss peace terms, he observed that 'if the British were tacitly allowed to introduce … a new principle [to put women and children into concentration camps] into warfare, that principle would establish a precedent'.[19]

The critics of the war had other concerns about the morality and the legality of the British tactics. This was particularly the case because the conflict began just a few months after the conclusion of the international Hague Peace Conference, which dealt with the laws and customs of war on land. The treaties and declarations were signed on 29 July and came into force on 4 September 1900. The Hague Convention was directly relevant to the war in

South Africa. Among the most substantial matters covered were those relating to the treatment of civilians caught up in conflict. The convention had greater authority because it gave formal international endorsement to the provisions of the International Declaration Concerning the Laws and Customs of War, which had been drafted and endorsed at an international conference held in Brussels in 1874. The provisions of both the 1874 conference and the 1899 convention are considered to have embodied the rules and customs of international law, and were ratified by the war crimes tribunals set up after the Second World War.

The 1899 provisions regarding non-combatants and their property were without ambiguity. Pillage was formally prohibited. Private property could not be confiscated. The pillage of a town, even when taken by assault was prohibited. Family honour and rights, individual lives and private property had to be respected. No general penalty, pecuniary or otherwise, could be inflicted on the population on account of the acts of individuals for which it could not be regarded as collectively responsible. Neither requisitions in kind, nor services, could be demanded from communities or inhabitants unless they were paid for.

The proceedings of the convention were regularly reported in the Australian newspapers, but there is no indication that during the middle months of 1899 there were any public figures who thought the provisions had any direct relevance to Australia. There was certainly some interest among the colonial churches, and information about the substance of the convention may have been quite widespread. In December 1901 a meeting was held in the small southern New South Wales town of Savernake. Regarded as a pro-Boer gathering, it was reported in both the *Sydney Morning Herald* and the *Times* in London. The first motion, moved and seconded by two Irish-Australians, read:

> That this meeting strongly opposes the despatch of more Australians to assist in the war against the Boers: that we object, even at the request of the British Government, to take part in depriving a brave and free people like the Boers of the liberty and independence which we ourselves enjoy and value so highly, or to assist in farm-burning, dam-cutting, and the general destruction of the property of the Boers, non-combatants as well as combatants, and the barbarous treatment of women and children … such methods being in direct violation of the rules of civilised warfare as laid down by the Hague conference, as well as an outrage on the principles of humanity and justice.[20]

Clearly, much of the action pursued by the imperial army during the second part of the war was, as Savernake's citizens declared, in direct contravention of the provisions of the 1899 convention and can, therefore, be considered as war crimes – as they were understood at the time and certainly as they are now. Australia's complicity in the infamy is beyond doubt. The individual colonies remained staunch supporters of the war until the end of 1900, sending further contingents and giving absolute approval to the British government's determination to pursue the conflict until full capitulation had been imposed. The federal government followed the same policies without demur and with even less parliamentary dissent. The dominions generally showed no sympathy for those groups in Britain pushing for an early negotiated peace that would preserve Boer independence.

But the complicity extends beyond the governments to the individual soldiers. Australians participated in the pillage and destruction of Boer farms, houses and villages. They dragged women and children from their homes and escorted them to the railway lines, where they were packed aboard uncovered wagons to be transported to the concentration camps. It is not clear how much of this brutal work was ever reported in Australia. But soldiers' own accounts contain abundant evidence of their involvement in the attendant atrocities.

One of the best sources for the activities of individual soldiers is a collection of reminiscences and diary entries collected in Tasmania soon after the war by John Bufton and published as *Tasmanians in the Transvaal War*. Bufton does not appear to have exercised any form of censorship of the kind almost certainly common in newspaper reports, imposed either by the correspondents themselves or by the subeditors in Australia. There is nothing to suggest that the Tasmanian troops behaved any differently from their comrades from the other colonies. Stealing seems to have been the favourite pastime of the young soldiers. In a letter to Bufton, a trooper in the Second Imperial Bushmen wrote that 'the most honest man in civil[ian] life will become the biggest thief on active service, and the Tasmanians generally were no exception to the rule'. In fact, they 'seemed to delight in stealing anything that came in sight'.[21] The insistent 'commandeering', as several diarists called it, was carried on in the Cape Colony as well as in the Transvaal. One man's series of diary entries listed the contraband taken in Victoria West:

> Plenty of commandeering going on – pigs and fowls … 'Commandeered' two fowls … Commandeered a case of biscuits, and in afternoon case of condensed milk … I commandeered a little teapot this evening … G.B. commandeered a case of meats, and Sergeant A. a case of port wine … One of the boys commandeered a case of Jewish Passover bread …[22]

The action was much more serious in the Boer republics, as a selection of diary entries will show:

> All Dutch houses passed were looted, and the families brought along … It was a very amusing sight to see our troops returning to camp with all kinds of loot, from a fully-saddled horse down to a fowl, and back again … a large number of women and children may be counted in our list of captures … we burnt all their houses … As usual [the firewood] was portion of a Dutch farmhouse, I having a book-case, glass door frame. Had great fun when 'burring' things up, breaking glass, cracking wood, hammering etc.; made a great noise. All went out skirmishing yesterday looking through houses, etc., several of which were burnt down …

> A party of 20 went out on patrol to burn a house.
>
> This [house] we looted and burned to the ground …
>
> On an extra good day, goats, pigs, geese, turkeys, etc., on nearly every saddle.
>
> We have been marching round and round, burning and destroying …
>
> went out burning houses down, and had a little fighting with the enemy …
>
> we looted the place, taking everything we could lay our hands [on] we lived on [sic] luxury for a few days the last week we have been destroying all we can get hold of it is the only way to deal with them.[23]

A trooper from the Second Imperial Bushmen gave Bufton an extract from a letter he had sent home describing the looting of a Boer general's farm, explaining,

> we looted everything he had a big engune [sic] that he used to grind his flour with we smashed it to pieces we got a fine lot of dryed [sic] fruit of all descriptions and jam and butter eggs some got a bit of money bedding and clothes any quantity of them the officers got some fine pictures we could have got some but we had no where to carry them one picture was of old Kruger and his royl [sic] family I bet it cost fifty pounds.[24]

A diarist described the raid on another Boer officer's farm. In less than twenty minutes the place was a 'perfect wreck'. Some of the men hacked 'a grand piano to pieces for their camp fires', others 'found a quantity of jewellery and other curios'.[25] Another diarist described the raid on the farm of a member of the Botha family. The matriarch was away when the soldiers arrived and they ransacked the whole house. When she returned and 'saw the house with everything upside down, she wept very bitterly'. The officer in charge ordered that everything be returned. It apparently had little effect, the diarist recording his loot: 'I got three fowls, one duck, one coloured rug, photo of "Big Ben," four spoons, two knives, one fork and a gridiron'. They had, he noted, 'a thoroughly enjoyable day'.[26] On other occasions the Tasmanians went on destructive rampages in the Northern Cape, which was not enemy territory. At Carnarvon they took 'charge of a bar and [broke] things up a good deal'. A month later they were in trouble again and got 'into row' for looting a town and a general hospital.[27]

Looting was one thing: shooting prisoners was quite another, and had been especially forbidden in the declaration of 1874 and the convention of 1899. A trooper diarist mentioned several incidents quite casually:

> August 28th. – Two native spies were shot this afternoon; was detailed for firing party, but missed it.
>
> September 1st. – Eight Boers captured and shot, and later on three more got a free ticket for 'Kingdom Come,' as one trooper said.[28]

It is impossible to know how common the practice was, but this young Tasmanian obviously did not think the shooting he recorded was exceptional.

The reports that Australians read in their papers emphasised the achievements of their soldiers, both real and exaggerated. There was already a tradition of picturing the troopers as manifesting peculiarly Australian characteristics. Though many men came from urban areas, the emerging legend suggested that they were natural horsemen, inured to hard outdoor living, capable of living off the land and able to find their way across country. These ideas were working their way into the speeches of politicians by the first year of the war and into the innumerable addresses delivered whenever a new detachment departed or a group of veterans returned. The British played up to these antipodean fancies, but their private assessment was that the colonial volunteers were more trouble than they were worth. Douglas Haig, then a senior cavalry officer, believed that most volunteers should go home. They strained resources so greatly 'that the army was bogged down and victory delayed'.[29]

By any measure the colonial engagement was an unnecessary war. As well, it illustrated the difficulty of knowing in advance how and when a mission would end; it lasted much longer and involved far more men than anyone envisaged in October 1899. The dominion troops performed well enough to satisfy the vanity of communities with little experience of war, but they were never a decisive factor in the defeat of the Boers. What, then, was gained? How did Australia benefit by the loss of more than 600 young lives? Were the consequent bereavement and grief worthwhile? Did anyone bother to actually compute the scale of the loss in terms of premature death and loss of future productivity? Was war thought to be exempt from the normal quotidian calculation of profit and loss? What, after all, was the point in gratuitously adding to the torment of the Afrikaner people, whom most Australians had to concede presented no possible threat to the country? Were overseas critics right? Did the colonies go to war light-heartedly, as Olive Schreiner believed? Did loyalty to Britain take the place of thought and reflection, as the American Reinsch insisted? Were there Australian leaders who believed the experience of war was usefully instructive, that war was inherently a good thing, that the nation itself was better off in 1902 than in 1899?

RS Skirving, an Australian army surgeon, wrote after his time in South Africa that war was a vast but not an unmixed evil. In fact, he knew 'of no better remedy for individual and national selfishness, no greater moral tonic'. Without war Australia would become a nation 'without chivalry, without national courage, and without patriotism which is the finest form of unselfishness'.[30] But what was probably more persuasive than the doctor's social Darwinism was the belief, often expressed both in 1885 and during the Boer War, that Australia had come of age and joined the nations of the world. Did some Australians feel better about their country in the aftermath of the South African intervention? Did they walk taller believing that the country had punched above its weight?

Imperial leaders had reason to be pleased with the dominion involvement. It certainly mollified the sense of international isolation and was a useful counter to the criticism from British liberals and Irish nationalists. But there was more to it than that. Chamberlain was delighted with the way it had turned out. The enthusiastic response was the most telling endorsement of the ideas of greater Britain and imperial federation. He had said all along that there were two ways to bring about imperial integration. One was commerce, the other war. Trade reform was much harder to effect, as he was to learn shortly after the war. And the need for tariff reform was never pressing, whereas the need to augment imperial military manpower was critical in the absence of unachievable conscription. The military planners had been single-minded in their intention to entice the dominions into their strategic plans since before the Boer War, and to establish permanent forces that could be accessed by the imperial government to fight anywhere in the world. They were engaged in a process of martial grooming that achieved its most spectacular confirmation when the dominions plunged into war in 1914. The experience on the veldt both underlined Britain's military weakness and enhanced the value of the dominion forces. If there was an imperial desire to head off dominion nationalism – or separatism as it was often called – the Boer War was extraordinarily successful.

In Australia there was a dramatic turning away from that tradition that incorporated, in varying strengths, republicanism, isolation, neutrality and even continental defence. It was a decisive confirmation of the alternative way of imperial loyalty, racial solidarity and both collective and forward defence. It projected Australia on a specific path with such momentum that it has not been left for more than a hundred years. The way became so familiar that the existence of an alternative route was widely forgotten.

There was little evidence that the veterans or the political leaders who sent them away had retrospective regrets about involvement. Australians showed little interest in reflecting on the morality of what had been done. That is until early 1904, when the news broke that the imperial authorities had decided to bring more than 60 000 Chinese contract labourers into the Transvaal to work in the goldmines of the Rand. Australian politicians were outraged. Dead children were one thing, Chinese labour quite another. They generally had a visceral hatred of Chinese workers and had passed the Immigration Restriction Act to make sure that nothing of the kind could ever be tried in Australia. But many had supported the war because of the reported harsh treatment of the largely British workers or uitlanders. The importation of Chinese labour was an affront to Australian opinion but was pursued by the imperial administration of the Transvaal in order to revive the local war-ravaged economy. One of the great ironies of the situation was that the mine owners were wary of employing a large white workforce, fearing the emergence of a powerful labour movement of the kind that had evolved in Australia and to which the presence of the colonial forces had alerted them.

Members of the federal parliament gave vent to their anger during a long debate stretching over three nights in March 1904. The common view was that the introduction of Chinese labour undermined the reasons for Australian involvement in the first place. The most immediate question that had motivated the Australian colonies to intervene was the status of the foreign and mainly British workers on the Rand. Beyond that was the desire to achieve British predominance in the whole of South Africa, which was to be secured by the large-scale migration of English and colonial workers. 'We were told', Alfred Deakin declared,

> at the outbreak of hostilities in South Africa, that it was a war for the miners of the Transvaal. If the authorities had gone on to say it was a war for Chinese miners, what a different aspect it would have worn. We were told also that it was a war for the enlargement of the franchise, and to secure increasing self-governing powers. But whose franchise? The Chinese franchise? Whose self-governing powers? The self-governing powers of Asiatics? Why were we not told of this outcome at the commencement of the struggle? We should then have said – 'Keep your mines; your cheapness is too dearly purchased. It is not to be bought with blood.'[31]

After 1904, few Australians continued to defend the decision to become involved in the war. In Britain it became a liability for the Conservative–Unionist government. Joseph Chamberlain resigned as Colonial Secretary in 1903 over trade and tariff policy. The Liberal Party swept to power with a record majority early in 1906. Many of the so-called pro-Boers were in the new ministry. David Lloyd George, the most vehement opponent of the war, became president of the Board of Trade and treasurer from 1908. In South Africa itself, the expected postwar hegemony of the British population never eventuated, and after the creation of the Union in 1909, the Boer generals Botha, Hertzog and Smuts came to power, which they continued to exercise for the next forty years.

There was an interesting exchange about the war in the Australian Senate in 1904, during a debate on a defence bill. Queensland Senator John Mullan announced: 'I condemned the South African War as an unjust war, and as one of the biggest blots in the history of the Empire'. His colleague Senator Henry Turley interjected: 'Every one does that now'.[32]

Well perhaps not everyone, but it became progressively harder for Australians to justify their South African venture. After the First World War it was largely forgotten, and monuments all over the nation were disregarded or fell into disrepair. Which means it is necessary to explain the renewed and almost totally uncritical contemporary interest in the infamous war on the veldt.

10

The nation's selective memory

In 2002 the Australian War Memorial published a book to mark the centenary of the end of the Boer War in May 1902, entitled *Australia's Boer War: The War in South Africa, 1899–1902*.[1] The author, historian Craig Wilcox, looked back on the way the war had been viewed during that hundred years. He observed that after 1902, Commonwealth governments, moved 'either by disenchantment or indifference', failed to arrange for any commemoration of the war. There was no South Africa Day after 1902, no national war memorial or official history. Australia, he remarked, had shrugged off an event that, at the time, had seemed so important, so compelling.[2]

How different things have been since 2002! The war

has been swept up in Australia's swelling carnival of commemoration. There has been no sign of that erstwhile indifference or disenchantment. There were private and localised commemorations of the war after 2002.There was a small industry that saw the publication of many books, often privately, on almost every aspect of the Australian involvement. But the cause became both official and national when, in 2006, a decision was made to provide a site at the bottom of Anzac Avenue in Canberra for a Boer War memorial, which was both dedicated and blessed on what has become known as Boer War Day, 31 May 2008. Four years later the design for the memorial was unveiled in Canberra by the chief of the Defence Force, General David Hurley. It depicted four bronze, life-sized mounted troopers, galloping through the low bush of the Highveld landscape.[3] The campaign to raise money for the memorial was spearheaded by the National Boer War Memorial Association, which held its inaugural meeting at Victoria Barracks in Sydney in February 2011. In the following year the association organised the first rally of Boer War descendants. Other rallies have followed. Memorabilia has been crafted for sale, including a smart tie in blue, red and yellow stripes – the colours of the Queen's Boer War medal – as well as distinctive badges, pens and key rings. The most expensive item is a laser-etched crystal ice-bucket modelled after a military side drum. The Royal Australian Mint went one better in 2014, issuing a fifty-cent memorial coin. The attendant publicity announced that the coin was created as a tribute to those who had served in the Boer War, 'defending the lives and honour of British subjects in South Africa'. It was to be a symbol of 'history, commitment, tradition and pride'. That was all very well, but the mint ventured further into historical interpretation, declaring that 'overwhelmingly', Boer guerrillas were 'outnumbered and conquered by Australian troops'.[4]

The first official ceremonies were held in more than fifty towns and cities in New South Wales at the end of May 2010, and the number of services and their geographical spread has increased every year since. Separate gatherings have been held to commemorate particular battles or to rededicate restored memorials to soldiers killed in South Africa. In the past few years, ceremonies have been held in all capital cities, and many provincial centres and suburbs. They have had impressive official endorsement from both military and civic leaders. Governors, leading politicians, mayors and aldermen shared platforms with military leaders, both active and retired, descendants of the warriors and, in many cases, students from local high schools and members of scout and guide troops. Historical enthusiasts have enlivened formal proceedings, riding in on horses while dressed in historic uniforms. The theme chosen for the 2015 ceremonies was 'Fathers of the ANZACS'. It was a motif that predisposed the many official speakers to celebrate the Boer War troops as founders of a tradition that has been followed ever since. That being so, it was necessary to avoid any serious assessment of the nature of the war itself. Founders and fathers had to be above reproach.

The official apotheosis had begun back in 2002, when a contingent of soldiers was sent to South Africa to participate in centenary commemorations. The Minister for

Veterans' Affairs at the time, Danna Vale, declared that:

> Those Australians who served in the Boer War began the fine military tradition that would be followed in wars and conflicts over the next century, from Gallipoli to the members of the Australian Defence Force serving today as part of the international coalition against terrorism.[5]

Since that time, the tradition has become entrenched and the hyperbole has flowered. In his Boer War Day message of 2015, read all over the country, Governor-General Sir Peter Cosgrove announced:

> These men and women were the first to serve Australia in battle, and they did us proud. Their knowledge of the bush, their riding ability, exceptional shooting skills and the medical attention they provided earned them universal respect, and their loyalty to each other forged the sense of solidarity that lives with our soldiers to this day. In a difficult war far from home, our Boer War veterans showed what it was to be an Australian. In this ANZAC centenary year, their deeds are as important and relevant as ever and they are widely regarded as the fathers of the ANZACS …[6]

The chief of the Defence Force, Air Chief Marshal MD Binskin, provided a similar message of support for the National Boer War Memorial Association, observing that it was in South Africa that Australian military forces were to first gain their reputation for 'dash, skill, mateship and courage in adversity – qualities that were to become synonymous with the Anzacs in the First World War and that we seek to instil in our military personnel today'.[7] The message from Prime Minister Tony Abbott was even more removed from the reality of the war on the veldt. Australians, he asserted,

> have always served to uphold the rights of the weak against the strong, the rights of the poor against the rich and the rights of all to strive for the very best they can. We don't fight to conquer; we fight to help, to build and to serve.[8]

One has to wonder if the prime minister's speechwriter knew anything, or even cared at all, about the Boer War.

We have, then, a strange paradox. Interest in the war has been revitalised. The history of the conflict has assumed an importance it hasn't had for a hundred years. And yet the focus is so constricted, the curiosity so contained. So much is left unacknowledged or at least unsaid. In all the many commemorative speeches, the subject matter has remained the same. Audiences are told again and again about the fighting qualities of our own soldiers and the sacrifice of those who didn't return. It is as though South Africa merely furnished the location and the occasion for the birth of a national military tradition. The distinguished historian Geoffrey Blainey wrote that South Africa provided a 'training ground for Gallipoli and other campaigns in the First World War'.[9] The government's official online account of the war announces that the Australians' reputation for bravery, toughness and cool-headedness was the 'foundation for the Australian warrior image that later became the ANZAC legend of World War I'. The Australian army celebrates its birthday each year on 1 March, in remembrance of the moment when the various contingents in South Africa were absorbed into the new national force.

The war also provided an opportunity for Australia to 'define its identity'.[10] Although the conflict was an event of international significance, Australian commentators adopt a nationalistic outlook that verges on solipsism. This was a common characteristic of accounts written during the war itself. Did our men measure up? Were they good soldiers? An even more persistent question was, were they admired and respected by their comrades from other armies? Did the British authorities appreciate their true value? Intimations of this narrow nationalism can be found in contemporary writing. Wilcox's official history is an admirable book, but it sits comfortably within the school of patriotic commentary. He observes that while there were never enough Australians to influence the course of the war, 'they punched above their weight' and outshone their counterparts in Britain's Imperial Yeomanry.[11] The South African war, Wilcox declares, 'was a good war for Australia'.[12]

Do the Australians who gather on Boer War Day believe it was a good war? Do they think the soldiers did us proud? Do the many families who now claim kin with long-forgotten veterans of the conflict know anything about the horror of the war? Do they concern themselves with the terrible impact on Boer civilians, mainly women and children?

Official histories make relevant, albeit oblique references. Wilcox observed that the Australians 'could be even more heavy-handed and cruel than the army's strategy required' – a pertinent comment, but scarcely revealing.[13] The official government website notes that the war saw 'the use of guerrilla tactics that destroyed the lives and homes of civilians'.[14] This is an even more opaque observation. But as with so much of present-day commentary, it deftly avoids the true infamy of the Boer War and Australia's complicity in it.

More particularly, the reputation of the Australian soldiers is carefully shielded. This is done so effectively that few people are aware of their direct involvement in the terrorising of Boer civilians, the burning, looting and indiscriminate destruction. They were also complicit in the truly shocking consequences of the imprisonment of women, children and the elderly in concentration camps. Both at the time and now, a century later, this vast crime against humanity has been treated with an easy insouciance in Australia. It might give us some pause to realise that four or five times more prisoners died in British camps than the number of Australian captives who died at the hands of the Japanese in the Second World War. And the victims were overwhelmingly women and children. Do we ever face up to the truly horrifying fact of the 30 000 dead children? Olive Schreiner accused the Australians of going to war in a light-hearted fashion. Is that the way we now commemorate our complicity?

What does this do to the reputation of the fathers of the ANZACS? Do we still claim them as the founders of our warrior tradition? Did they show us what it means to be an Australian, as the governor-general believes? Did this, of all wars, allow Australians to define their identity? Should we really be proud of punching above our weight in such an infamous war? Try as we may, these are questions that will never go away. And maybe this was why governments in the years before the First World War chose not to dwell on the South African venture. If, as a nation, we are determined to disinter the Boer War warriors, they will emerge clad in infamy. How could it be otherwise?

Australians are clearly adept at choosing those aspects of war that enhance the heroic, albeit humane image of our soldiers while eschewing the rest. And this relates to the utterly distinctive nature of Australia's war history. The country has been at war many times, but all the fighting has been overseas. The community at large has had no direct experience of war, and distance has both mollified the attendant horrors and eased the task of the ever-active censors. Australians have been told what was thought good for them and what they liked to hear. The army in particular has adopted the stance of our sporting teams – what happens on tour stays on tour. Community innocence and ignorance allow the burnished image of the soldier to remain unstained.

It helps, too, that most of Australia's wars have been fought beside Britain or the United States in places and against enemies not of our own choosing. The big political and strategic decisions were made far away in London or Washington, often with little input from Australia. This had the unintended consequence of allowing Australia to avoid hard moral and legal questions about the necessity and validity of each conflict, to share in the glory when things went well but avoid the opprobrium if and when interventions lost their lustre. Without a direct hand in the political calculus, Australians could concentrate on the performance of our soldiers. And with the politics left out, the suffering and sacrifice could be seen to have a purity of purpose not measurable by demonstrable national benefit. Who would stoop to cost-benefit assessment when heroes stalked the land? Without strategic calculation, war could indeed become like an exalted kind of sport in which the mettle of men and nations was tested. The central question became how they fought, not why they fought.

These characteristics were already apparent in some of the Boer War literature. WT Reay was one of the Australian correspondents, writing for the Melbourne and Adelaide dailies. In his 1900 book *Australians in War*, he wrote that the war was the 'test of our powers as a nation … and the test was borne faithfully and well'. War was the 'great testing and convincing ground … in the face of a keenly observant world'.[15] But as he explained to his readers,

> I have nothing to do here with what may be called the 'politics' of the war. Like every other British citizen, I claim the right to hold opinions on that head, but would invite all classes of readers to sink political considerations for the time, and turn their minds to the phases of the matter with which alone this work deals – to the actual doings of our citizen soldiers.[16]

The upsurge of interest in the Boer War is one manifestation of what has been called the militarisation of Australian history. For the last twenty years, Australian governments have funded an intense program to commemorate the importance of our military history. It is quite unprecedented. No other aspect of national history has ever received such lavish support, channelled as it is through the Australian War Memorial and the Department of Veterans' Affairs. There seems to be an endless flow of funds. The whole project has always received enthusiastic bipartisan support in the parliament. Consequently, the campaign has reached into every part of the country. Books, films and research projects have been subsidised. Communities have been encouraged to apply for grants to fund local projects. As a result, old neglected monuments have been refurbished and new ones built. Young trees have been planted in ageing avenues of honour. New days of remembrance have been added to an already crowded calendar of commemoration. Governors, military and political leaders spend an unprecedented amount of time pinning on their medals, laying wreaths and making earnest speeches about past wars. They now attend the funerals of fallen servicemen with a regularity that was never expected of them in the past. Politicians seek to draw on the resurgent prestige of the armed forces. The ready availability of newly digitised service records has fused family and military history in a way not possible before. All over the country, families seek out ancestors who fought in the wars of the early 20th century and proudly claim relatives they often knew nothing about. Even distant cousins and completely forgotten great-uncles are woven into family sagas.

Children have been assiduously courted to join the cavalcade. Schools across the nation have been bombarded with free, professionally developed curriculum material, including films, books, compact discs and posters. Subsidies are available for trips to Canberra, where visits to the War Memorial are mandated because tour organisers are told that is where young people will learn what it means to be an Australian. Brendan Nelson, current head of the memorial, makes an even larger claim. His institution, he believes, is the soul of the nation.[17] Nationwide essay competitions reward winners with fully funded tours of Gallipoli and European battlefields. There is little reticence or embarrassment among the military propagandists. They openly canvass the need to reach out to children from the earliest years of primary school with their message about the central role of war in the national experience. Their crusade seems to be closer to propaganda than pedagogy. And the sanctity accorded all consideration of fallen countrymen stands in the way of doubt or dissidence.

The inevitable consequence of such an enduring, handsomely funded campaign to commemorate the nation's military history is that all other aspects of the national story are overshadowed and thereby diminished. They have never received the official patronage now bestowed on the historiography of war. This works its way into the research that is funded and the institutions that benefit. Two of Canberra's museums illustrate the disparity. They face one another across Lake Burley Griffin. The Museum of

Democracy in the old parliament house receives a pittance in comparison with the bountifully funded Australian War Memorial. And yet Australia's contribution to the history of democracy is by any measure more distinctive than its involvement in overseas wars. And the evolution of our institutions and our manners unfolded here on Australian soil. So the endless cavalcade of military commemoration has seriously distorted the nation's history. This may not be apparent or even matter to young people, but many older Australians find it a deeply disturbing development.

Anzac stands at the centre of the cult of the digger. This truth was powerfully reaffirmed with the commemorations for the centenary of the Gallipoli landing in April 2015. Massive funding ensured that the related events in both Turkey and Australia were on a heroic scale. Rhetoric flowed as freely as government funding. The same message was reinforced in speeches delivered all over the continent and beyond. The ceremonies were conducted to pay tribute to all of the country's war dead, but there was, as always, much more to it than that. The campaign on the Gallipoli Peninsula has a greater hold on the national imagination than a homely lament for the dead. The loss of life was unprecedented in 1915, though soon to be overshadowed by the casualties on the Western Front. But what really matters is the additional dimension given to the landing, which has often been described as the most significant event in Australian history. And the massive publicly funded ceremonies were a manifestation of this perceived significance. Anyone who has talked to school students on the subject of Anzac will come away with the unmissable impression that the central message about Gallipoli has been most effectively implanted in the minds of the next generation. Both the rhetoric of the speechmakers and the comments of young people confirm that Gallipoli was no ordinary event. It both made and defined Australia as a nation. And the young men who died did so in order for Australia to be free.

It is hard to know where to begin. How does sober historical assessment confront heroic, nationalistic myths? But as we have seen, the idea that the nation was made or came of age in war had been around for thirty years by 1915. It was what serious men said about the Sudan campaign in 1885. It was repeated much more insistently in 1899 and 1900 as the colonial contingents sailed for South Africa. The idea was already well worn in 1915. But the repetition is illustrative. During the late 19th and early 20th centuries, many people in Europe and North America strongly believed that war was a beneficial tonic that kept nations vividly alive, avoiding the degenerative effect of long periods of peace. There was also the powerful influence of social Darwinism, which suggested that nations, like species in the natural world, needed to respond to challenges in order to survive the relentless and unavoidable struggle for existence. It was a heady, dangerous intellectual cocktail. Australia shared these ideas. It was not at all exceptional to think in 1914 that nations were made in war, which was the supreme test for individuals and societies alike. What is truly astonishing is that these long discredited and discarded ideas survive in Australia and are embodied in the most important national ceremonies and passed on almost as holy writ to our children. The belief that war was a creative force in society was abandoned in many countries as a result of the First World War, surviving only in Nazi Germany, Imperial Japan and fascist Italy. It did not survive the horrors of the Second World War. All of which raises the important question of its survival in Australia, embalmed in the rhetoric given birth by the Gallipoli landing.

The central proposition falters when placed beside the situation that existed before 1915 and what was to follow. What was the young Australia lacking at the start of 1914 that was provided by a landing on the shores of the Ottoman Empire at the behest of the imperial government in pursuit of goals that were unknown to Australian leaders? What is more exceptional is the implication that in a few months of fighting at Gallipoli the young men achieved what had been beyond the reach of the many thousands of Australians who built homes, businesses and institutions in the generations leading up to the war. It carries with it the suggestion that soldiers are more creative than civilians, the bayonet mightier than the plough. It contains the implication that war is more formative than peace, that warriors are more important than legislators or administrators. And then there are the events that followed Gallipoli. War did not create and it certainly did not unite the nation. In fact, Australia was deeply divided by war. Class and religious fissures were torn wide open. Loyalty to the empire intensified in many minds and remained strong for the postwar generation. Empire frequently outbid nation. So much had been sacrificed in the name of King and empire that neither could be questioned without betraying the thousands who did not return. It was symptomatic of the postwar generation that Western Australia voted by a two to one majority to break away from the Federation in 1933 and return to the status of a Crown colony.

What has happened to Australia? How do we explain the current obsession with war? While seeking an explanation, we could do no better than turn to those opponents of the involvement in the Boer War who were concerned that Australia was in danger of succumbing to militarism. They had witnessed the popular enthusiasm for war, the official embrace of the imperial refusal to consider a negotiated settlement, and the concomitant insistence on annexation and complete Boer capitulation. The anti-war cause in Australia lacked the galaxy of prominent intellectual and cultural figures that took up the fight in Britain. This raises the thought that there was less institutional and cultural resistance to war in Australia than in the imperial heartland, that the Gladstonian tradition had not travelled well. But the type of militarism that men like HB Higgins feared failed to emerge. Australia did not develop a distinctive military caste associated with the aristocracy in the way that was still common in Europe in 1901. The local tradition of the citizen soldier was quite different. Even so, the Australian army was not a democratic institution. It was strictly hierarchical and authoritarian. There has always been much sentimental talk of the diggers' irreverence and refusal to salute, but they had to obey the orders of their superior officers or face often severe punishment. And the military hierarchy mirrored and accentuated the class structure of civil society. So we have the little noticed paradox latent in the cult of the digger that democratic, egalitarian Australians performed their most heroic feats while under the heavy constraints of enforced obedience.

The militarisation of our history is having other consequences that reach beyond our reflections on the past. It has begun to impact on public life and to change political practice. This became apparent with the coming to power of the Abbott Coalition government. Refugee policy was particularly affected. The Customs service and the Department of Immigration have become militarised. The paramilitary Australian Border Force was launched in July 1915. Operation Sovereign Borders has turned the refugee problem into one that threatens national sovereignty and demands a military response headed by a retired senior officer. Proceedings in the Arafura Sea are treated like a military campaign and cloaked in the secrecy reserved for such undertakings. The resulting lack of accountability removes the whole exercise from scrutiny by the parliament and the media. The Minister for Immigration in the Abbott government, Scott Morrison, was in the habit of appearing at press conferences flanked by a senior military officer, deliberately smudging the distinction between civil and military authority. There were many other pertinent examples. Prime Minister Abbott was constantly accompanied by senior military or Federal Police officers. Retired officers were routinely appointed to carry out missions that in the past would have been assigned to diplomats or senior bureaucrats. Ministers clearly seek to draw on the prestige now accorded the military, which helps shield them from the sort of scrutiny to which politicians are normally subjected. A young war hero was recently appointed to the chair of the Australia Day Council. As an eminent citizen, Peter Cosgrove was a popular choice for the role of governor-general, but given its timing, the appointment was a further example of the growing intrusion of the military into political life. And when that happens, democracy is diminished.

The heroic standing accorded the warriors of past wars influences debate about conflict in general, and about war today. The tradition of the digger stretches unbroken from the Boer War to the present. Its durability ensures its current compacted vigour. Commemoration of past wars projects their lustre forward into the present. The habit of focusing on how Australians fought, rather than why they did so, influences current debates.

It is instructive to consider the aftermath of the Second Gulf War. In the United States and in Britain there has been an intense debate about what is now seen as a disastrous misadventure. Both George Bush and Tony Blair were subjected to severe and searching criticism, loss of respect and impaired authority. An official inquiry into Britain's involvement continues at the present moment. How different the postwar situation was in Australia. John Howard experienced none of the opprobrium visited on his military partners. There has been no inquiry into the reasons for Australian involvement, its cost or its value, despite the estimated expenditure of $5 billion. The illegality of the war, which is openly discussed overseas, finds little purchase here. We don't even publicly discuss whether the involvement was worthwhile, and there seems to be little sense that Australia has any residual responsibility for the chaotic events that have followed the overthrow of Saddam Hussein. When the last troops returned in 2009, the then prime minister, Kevin Rudd, was asked if there would be an enquiry into the Australian involvement. He said no. His reason was instructive. He explained that it would be inappropriate to do so while the soldiers were settling back into civilian life. Much the same can be said about the involvement in Afghanistan, which came to an end after thirteen years in December 2014. More than 30 000 service personnel served there. Forty-one Australians were killed and 260 wounded. The overall cost was $9.3 billion. It appears that no review has been conducted into whether the intervention was worthwhile.[18]

The shadow of militarism has not lifted. It is clear that Australian governments are able to go to war with an ease that is both dangerous and unusual in a democracy. We have inherited the British constitutional practice of devolving power over war, peace and treaties to the Crown, with no necessity for parliamentary veto or even input. Various attempts to bring war-making powers within the reach of the legislature have achieved nothing. In the United States, the relevant presidential powers are shared with the Senate. In Britain, decisions about war are brought to the Commons for debate. The experience of involvement in Afghanistan and Iraq suggests that Australian governments suffer no penalty from sending troops overseas, regardless of the outcome. Criticism of wars can be construed as cowardly attacks on the men and women on the frontline. Their prestige shields politicians from legitimate scrutiny. It was not surprising, then, that Tony Abbott sought to militarise the national response to the shooting down of a Malaysian airliner in July 2014, to the extent of proposing at one stage to send 1000 troops to Eastern Ukraine in the middle of a civil war. And the same can be said of the renewed and growing commitment to war in Iraq and Syria. It happened with an ease that was quite astonishing. The commitment was simply announced rather than debated. Parliament had no formal involvement. The Labor opposition was complicit in failing to ask hard questions or to refer back to our involvement between 2003 and 2009 and use that experience as guide and warning. Tony Abbott was never questioned, let alone called to account for his responsibility as a cabinet minister in 2003 for the disastrous consequences of the Second Gulf War.

In fact, the Coalition government has given the impression that it is keen on war and was pleased to be asked to become involved once again in the Middle East. It is a development foreshadowed by the then newly installed Minister for Defence, David Johnston, in an interview with a Fairfax reporter in September 2013 a few days after his appointment. He declared that he wanted the forces to be 'battle-ready' for future conflicts in the Middle East or south Asia. He predicted that Australian troops would likely need to go back there sometime in the future. He explained that after fourteen years of involvement in overseas conflicts, the defence forces had 'a strong fighting momentum that should not be lost'. After fourteen years of warfare it might have been thought that the country was ready for peace, but quite the contrary. War, it seemed, created both the desire and the need for future conflict. The minister wanted a war of his own. Indeed, he explained that he planned to maintain and 'augment our readiness' for future fights, observing that with the impending withdrawal from Afghanistan it was necessary to 'maintain some interest for the troops'. It was a truly extraordinary statement. The minister clearly took it for granted that there was need for Australian intervention on the other side of the world. He seemingly assumed that the country had the legal and moral right to do so whenever and wherever it pleased. The army was ready for action and should be given its head. A new war was required to maintain the interest of the troops. Perhaps the even more extraordinary aspect of these statements is that they passed largely unnoticed or at least unremarked, despite being the lead story in the *Sydney Morning Herald*.[19] Apparently, neither government nor opposition felt there was anything exceptional in the comments. They were the new minister's first public statements; they must presumably have been made in consultation with his department. As a long-time adviser to the prime minister on defence, Johnston must have known his first ministerial statement would sit comfortably with the outlook of fellow members of the new government.

Clearly, contemporary Australian governments find it easy to go to war, and suffer little as a result, even when the commitment costs both lives and treasure and has no measurable or demonstrable benefit for the nation. And the threshold they need to cross in order to send troops overseas is perilously low. This is how past and present meet. The ongoing commemoration has demonstrable consequences. While there are always ritualistic references to death and destruction, other messages prevail. There is never an assessment of why Australia has been so often involved in war, whether we have benefited or whether we would have been better off avoiding unnecessary wars. Young people must get the impression that war is a natural and inescapable aspect of national life. War is what we do and we are good at it. There are constant references in public discussion to the assertion that we 'punch above our weight'. Our militarism manifests itself in the way we speak, as though war provides the occasion for the display of heroism and military virtuosity regardless of why we are involved in the first place. And while there is much talk of dying – or more usually of sacrifice – there is little mention of killing, and never any public assessment of the carnage visited on distant countries in our name. There is also a complete absence of any discussion of our moral responsibility for death and damage. There is certainly no hint of that sense of concern, found in the work of Richard Cobden, about the infamy of involvement in unnecessary war.

The phrase 'Lest we forget' is the most revered one in national discourse, but the current enhanced awareness of past conflicts, reaching back to the Boer War, may be making it more rather than less likely that the same pattern will be repeated over and over again. Australians face the prospect that our children and grandchildren will, in the words of the American poet Robert Lowell, 'fall in small war on the heels of small war – until the end of time to police the earth ...'[20]

11

Dangerous allies or great and powerful friends?

The American alliance, the Cold War and the Vietnam involvement sparked renewed interest in the linked questions of national independence, continental defence and armed neutrality. Many of the issues, and the arguments as well, had been discussed before on numerous occasions. The continuity is, after all, not surprising. During the 20th century, the world moved relentlessly on and yet so much has remained the same. Geography is, as ever, the bedrock. Size and location are still the starting points for strategic assessment. Australia has no land borders to patrol and defend. There are no adjacent ancestral enemies or any external power with competing historical claims over the continent. Seaborne invasion remains, as it has been for 200 years, a daunting challenge for any potential aggressor. So the big questions endure.

The men who debated the appropriate role for the country in 1900 would quickly recognise today's contentions. How independent should the country be? How independent could it be? Should international relations be dominated by a great and powerful friend? Would such a relationship drag Australia into unnecessary wars? Where should Australian forces fight and why? Should defence of the continent itself stand above anything else?

Other developments would surprise the men of Federation. In the 21st century, Australians are more at ease with their Asian and Melanesian neighbours than were their grandparents and great-grandparents – but not entirely so. And these neighbours are vastly more consequential than they were a hundred years ago. The British Empire is no more, but habits learnt in its shadow linger. Australia is no longer a predominantly British society either demographically or culturally. The smooth segue from imperial loyalty to American republican embrace, however, obviated the need for national reassessment of the habit of dependence or a weighing-up of its costs and benefits. The generations of imperial loyalists were never called to account for the damaging consequences of decades of deference.

Contemporary Australia appears to be obsessed with war. National commemoration of the First World War surpasses what is being done anywhere else. Money seems to be no object. It has been estimated that the country is spending more than any other nation and possibly more than most other countries combined.[1] One of the most expensive follies is the museum and interpretative centre in northern France costing $100 million. How that sum would help underfunded museums in Australia! But it is not just the scale of funding that is distinctive. The focus of the commemoration is inimitably Australian. Battles and campaigns attract the most attention. From there interest focuses on the travails and sacrifice of the individual warrior. There is little movement in the other direction, from the battlefield to the embassies and chancelleries, from tactics to strategy and on to the questions of what the battles were really about and what, if anything, they achieved. Australia, it seems, prefers its commemoration of war with the politics extracted.

This Australian habit of ignoring the politics of war serves two purposes. It purifies war, easing the apotheosis of the warrior. And with the grand strategy removed it becomes difficult to draw up an account of what was achieved and whether it was worth the loss and suffering. War can simply be about fighting, and we do that well. So it seems that the more we talk about war, the less we can judge whether war in general, or particular campaigns, were really necessary wars as far as Australia was concerned. The cult of the digger stands in the way of sceptical assessment. Doubt dissolves when met by communal and personal reverence for individual suffering and sacrifice.

But doubts did emerge again in the 1980s. One of the most prominent, and certainly the most eloquent advocates of armed neutrality, was the distinguished writer David Martin.[2] He was the executive director of the Australian Association for Armed Neutrality between 1987 and 1990. Martin rested his case on a number of strongly related premises. Australia had the human and material resources to defend the continent, including the capacity to manufacture many military items that it didn't at the time produce. A potential invader would have to be able to land an army of as many as half a million on the Australian coast and supply it in a hostile environment. A landing in the north would still require a long trek to reach the Australian heartland. The country, he argued:

> certainly has the men, and could have the material, to deter any likely aggressor for as far as we can look ahead. She is one of the decreasing number of countries whose strategic frontiers still coincide with her national boundaries. Her material growth is keeping up with her neighbours. Time is not against her.[3]

But while Australia had the capacity to defend her own borders, she would never have the means or the right to intervene in the affairs of others or to try to prevent them 'alone or with allies, from following the political road of their own choosing'.[4] A key part of Martin's case was to call into question the common assumption that by wholeheartedly giving support to the United States we would obtain an implicit guarantee of assistance if we found ourselves threatened in the future. It was, he believed, a proposition resting on two insecure foundations. The first was that Australia could not defend itself. The second was that the United States would necessarily come to Australia's aid in all possible circumstances. If Australia were to forfeit American guarantees, Martin asserted, she would lose nothing either certain or vital.

In seeking relevant models for Australian neutrality, Martin, like numerous other advocates at the time, turned to countries like Sweden and Switzerland for instruction. He explained that what he proposed was 'a new policy and a new spirit', which he called a 'Scandinavian spirit'.[5] Oddly, neither Martin nor any of his supporters appeared to have had any knowledge of the domestic history of the ideas they promoted or an understanding of their provenance, which, as we have seen, reached back into the middle of the 19th century. They were not acquainted with the many public figures who had walked the same paths before them. It was an unfortunate deficiency, robbing modern debates of historical depth. There was a distinctive local tradition that would have added native vigour to their advocacy. Ideas of independence and neutrality were neither new nor exotic imports. The anthology of ideas articulated during many debates about the British Empire was highly relevant to the discussion in more recent times about the American alliance, despite the passage of time and the nature of the new protector.

Britain was (and the United States is now) a global power with ecumenical interests. To protect and defend those interests it needed to be able to project military power in every direction. That was a burden hard to escape. Conflict was a constant accompaniment of the assertion of control, even when the attendant rhetoric was about imposing peace or restoring order. The colonial critics of empire were adamant that close ties with Britain would be used to pull Australia into unnecessary wars in places little known or understood, against enemies who were no threat to the continental homeland. They were right to hold those fears. They were, like Cassandra, prescient but unappreciated. Their insight into the intrinsic violence of the imperial project is as relevant in the 21st century as it was in the 19th. Australia's tradition of fighting overseas, born, as we have seen, in the high summer of the British Empire, has been readily adapted to the demands of the United States.

In the late 19th century and early 20th century, Australian leaders found it hard to define their local identity and to distinguish imperial from national interests. They assumed that any challenge to the empire anywhere in the world was a threat to Australia. Even a blow to British prestige was a matter for local concern. Although living on an isolated continent they mentally inhabited an empire. This misplacement gave rise to one of the most exceptional characteristics of Australian history: the belief that the country should fight in places all over the world, that our interests are global, and that we therefore have the need as well as the moral and legal right to intervene anywhere and everywhere. From 1899 onwards, Australia showed a readiness to fight and an insouciance as to whether the involvement was justified or indeed worth the loss of life, the destruction, and the cost borne both by Australia itself and the countries that suffered from our interventions. War overseas has, over time, come to been seen as a normal rather than an exceptional feature of Australian life. Going to war as adjunct imperialists, accompanying a great and powerful friend, allowed Australia to engage in a recklessness about leaping into war. It was as though Australians felt safer fighting alongside a great power than living peacefully to themselves. And if the war turned out to be unsuccessful or ill conceived, Australia could always have the excuse that it really wasn't our war in the first place and that we were just helping out, that it wasn't our fault.

Australia's failure to truly weigh up the costs and benefits of membership of the British Empire after the disaster of Singapore in 1942 prepared the way for a similar uncritical devotion to the American alliance. The shock produced by what was called 'the great betrayal' created deeper dependence rather than stimulating a search for alternative policies. It was as though Australian leaders felt there was nowhere else to turn. But the idea of a fail-safe insurance policy was totally discredited in 1942, even though the Australians had been paying their premiums for the previous fifty years. The response was not what, in the circumstances, might have been expected. The conclusion was reached that what was needed was a different insurer rather than a new policy. So the great problems persist. There is still the vast disproportion in power, which renders ridiculous the idea of an alliance of equals. Australia remains a political and strategic mendicant. Australian leaders have clearly felt that they have to provide constant, uncritical support for American policies and ready involvement in her wars. All the Americans need do is foster the Australian illusion that there is a special relationship, which is not the case at all. There is an unwillingness to recognise now, as was the case before, that great powers have many complex and sometimes competing interests. And there is repetition, too, in the confusion of the relationships between states with those between individuals and families. Australians, to their cost, believed they had a filial relationship with Britain. National leaders now tell the country that the Americans are our mates – and perhaps some of them believe it, even though the relationship is based on the Anzus Treaty, which lacks any specific commitment beyond the need for consultation.

The central problem identified by the colonial critics of empire is still there. Imperial powers are prone to war. Dependent states feel an obligation to participate and, having done so once, establish a precedent that makes future involvement more rather than less likely. It is a dynamic identifiable as far back as the Sudan campaign and the Boer War. And willing allies become more useful if the war is unpopular at home and abroad. The more loyal the ally, the less they have to be considered. They can be taken for granted. As with Britain, so with America. Plans to train together, to coordinate command structures and standardise weapons, merely make future involvement more likely and easier to bring about. They do not add anything to the likelihood of future American involvement in the defence of Australia. And, as with the British Empire, the most likely scenario is that Australia will be expected to go to war with America's enemies whether or not the country has any quarrel with them of its own. A further problem is that it is hard for Australia to plan any alternative defence strategy. We cannot really know where the next engagement might be, who will be the designated enemy, how the war will be fought or what weapons will be required. There were few defence planners in 1991 who predicted that our armed forces were about to enter upon a generation-long military involvement in the Middle East. And all the while, continental defence remains out of fashion, and yet it provides the only way to calculate with reasonable certainty where and how we should have to fight.

The dramatic rise of China has initiated a new generation of contention about independence and neutrality. Historical parallels haunt the debate. To what extent is America's situation similar to Britain's at the time of Federation, facing the challenge of new rivals and in relative decline? Are the flawed interventions in the Middle East comparable with the Boer War, with its lesson about the limits of hegemonic power? Were Australia's recent and current interventions any more prudent or productive than the involvement in South Africa? Will they increase the likelihood of further military adventures? A question that currently troubles many minds is the similarity between the rapid contemporary rise of China and that of Germany a hundred years ago. There are worrying parallels. Can the existing powers, and the United States in particular, make room for the new rival?

China reacts against 150 years of humiliation and contemptuous dismissal by the West with what appears, to her, to be a necessary reassertion of her historical authority. The United States holds firmly to the idea of her exceptionalism. Rhetoric about being the greatest country in the world still fortifies the speeches of public figures from the president down to local office-bearers. And they mean it. Can such a country accept any threat to its predominance? Can China, for its part, tolerate the kind of containment clearly in the minds of many neighbouring powers, including, it would seem, Australia? Optimists argue that reason will prevail and that both sides recognise that war would be a disastrous outcome for two powers whose economies are now so interdependent. But here, too, there are echoes from the years leading up to the Great War. Perceptive critics used the argument even on the eve of war. Britain and Germany, they insisted, had become so economically integrated that war was no longer possible.

Australia faces the most difficult diplomatic situation ever. China is now of fundamental economic importance, but our military ties with the United States are drawn even tighter. Marines are now based in the Northern Territory. It was much easier to accept them than it would be to ask them to leave. Discussions are in train for the housing of strategic bombers in the country. All the indications are that the United States assumes that in the event of conflict with China, Australia will be there. No doubt their war plans take that for granted. A group of prominent critics despairs about the seemingly mindless drift of defence and foreign policy, and of the refusal to address the seriousness of the situation. No sitting federal politician appears willing to question the orthodoxy. Policy paralysis results.

Among the group of dissidents pressing for a fundamental reassessment of both policies and traditional attitudes, the most influential was undoubtedly the recently deceased one-time Liberal prime minister Malcolm Fraser, who, as we saw in chapter 1, in speeches, articles and a substantial book warned Australia about America, which he described as our dangerous ally.[6] He returned unrepentant to the subject just before his death:

> The closeness of our relationship with the United States, certainly in relation to the Pacific, means that we no longer have an independent capacity to stay out of America's wars under the policies that presently prevail in Australia … We have ceded Australian sovereignty, over matters of peace and war, to the United States. We have created a far more powerful linkage than ever existed in the days of Empire.[7]

In his book *Dangerous Allies*, Fraser surveyed, among other things, the history of the relationship between Britain and the Australian colonies in the days of empire. But like fellow critics of current policy, he showed no awareness of the anti-imperial tradition and of the ideas expressed in public meetings, journal articles and parliamentary addresses from as far back as the 1850s. And that's a pity. He would surely have admired the ideas and the forceful advocacy of that irascible, indefatigable Scot, John Dunmore Lang. It would have added cogency to his arguments if he had realised that his book was a notable contribution to a tradition of depth and substance. We can assume he would have appreciated the rhetoric of the progenitors he never knew. There was, for instance, Lang's declaration of the need to defend 'the land on which we dwell' and David Buchanan's determination to avoid overseas entanglements and instead 'stand upon this ground'. There were the anguished words of the Victorian Royal Commission in 1870, concerning the fate of dependencies that could 'influence the commencement or continuance of war no more than they can control the movements of the solar system'. There was the writer in *Tocsin* who feared that Australia would become a 'kennel of the foremost dogs of war'; and the worried words of George Reid, who observed that his colleagues were displaying a readiness to 'offer up our men upon any shrine of blood that offers itself'. As he developed his thesis, Fraser must have thought about the problem George Higinbotham posed for AI Clark: were the Australians willing to assume the burdens of independence? Perhaps he would have concluded that JA Hobson was right when he argued that independence presented 'rarer risks' than dependence on great and powerful friends.

We are able to observe how closely he trod in footprints he didn't know were there. His central argument is a close recapitulation of that of the anti-imperialists. Great powers are dangerous neighbours and perilous patrons, their talk of family loyalty and mateship notwithstanding. The colonial critics were certain that eventually Britain would drag Australia into a European war, which they realised would be a major conflagration. How prescient they were! We can only hope that Malcom Fraser is not so successful in the business of foretelling the future – that Australia's 21st century will not see a replay of the one just past, with its parade of unnecessary wars.

The adhesive power of empire, race and Crown remained undiminished until the middle of the 20th century. But had loyalty been worth it? Had it been a good investment in blood, treasure, emotional commitment and intellectual energy? It was by any measure a Sisyphean labour to attempt to preserve an ailing and ultimately doomed empire. Britain's heroic effort was to be expected. But how did Australia benefit? Australia's choice of empire over nation, already made in 1900, placed her on the wrong side of 20th-century history. Eschewing the nation, Australians became adjunct imperialists. And what a price they paid: 62 000 dead and 200 000 wounded in the First World War, 15 000 captured in Singapore in the Second. And they are just the largest entries in the ledger. Such accounting may appear nugatory – that was just the hand that Australia was dealt and there was nothing that could have been done about it. But Australia could have chosen independence or a more autonomous link with Britain, more like a normal alliance rather than the *faux* familial relationship sponsored by imperial loyalists, with its specious appeal to the fantasies of race and blood.

Japan's role in the First World War is instructive. Allied to Britain, the country met its treaty obligations and was rewarded with great power status at Versailles. Japan lost 600 men in the conflict or 1 per cent of the Australian death rate. As an independent country, Australia may still have chosen war in 1914 and 1939, but it would have meant fighting in different places in different ways. Or it may have followed the demands of so many colonial observers from JD Lang onwards, that the principal obligation of Australian forces was the defence of the homeland, that Australian foreign and defence policy be national rather than imperial, and that constant overseas interventions were bad in both principle and practice – as was killing people who didn't have to be our enemies and, like the Boers, could never threaten Australia. When, in the contemporary debate, doubt is cast upon the commitment to war in 1914, the response is that such a judgment reflects modern views rather than those at the time. But that ignores those critics in 19th-century Australia who warned that empire meant war and that Australia's commitment must be to continental defence.

The nationalist republican tradition deserves to be retrieved. It provides an alternative take on our history and a valuable tool for assessing current developments. We have no way of knowing how Australia would have fared as an independent nation-state in the turbulent years of the 20th century. We can only speculate. But the result could scarcely have been worse than the disasters brought upon us by the imperial loyalists. The empire was responsible for Australia's involvement in unnecessary wars that the nation needn't have fought. And while it is a worthy endeavour to remember those who were sacrificed to the cause, it would have been a better result if we didn't have to.

There is another way the critics of empire were prescient. Central to their arguments was that Australian geography was a strategic asset rather than a liability. In insisting that isolation, size and insularity were Australia's guarantor, not promises of protection from a great power, they were doubly prescient. Even at the high point of their march through South-East Asia, the Japanese did not seriously consider invading Australia.[8] And simultaneously, the British insurance policy upon which generations of imperialists had depended proved to be worthless. Even in retrospect, Australian historians have sympathised with the imperialists, arguing that they took a hard-headed attitude to Britain rather than a merely sentimental one, that they always had one eye on Australia's future security. But nothing is more intellectually and morally flaccid than failed realpolitik, particularly when the argument so often was that Australia should go to war to build up a bank of goodwill that could be drawn upon in some future crisis.

The central paradox remains. Australia has been consistently at war and is so again. And apart from the dark days of early 1942, it has never faced even the threat of invasion. The enemy has never been at the gate. Wars were not forced upon us. We freely chose to engage. We always had our reasons, but whether they justified going to war is another matter altogether. The perceived threats were usually speculative. They related to what might possibly happen sometime in the future. And in most cases the putative enemy would never have been able to present a possible threat to the homeland. The desire to assist a great and powerful friend may seem compelling at the time, but in retrospect appears to be far from sufficient justification for helping to carry war into countries we often know little about.

Two considerations arise. Has Australia gone to war too easily and too many times? Killing people to win favour with a powerful ally is scarcely the behaviour of an honourable nation. And have attitudes to conflict apparent since the Boer War encouraged our belligerence? More than that – have they meant that there are insufficient restraints to stay the dogs of war? Perhaps we have lacked a tradition that construes war as an exceptional tool of statecraft to be used sparingly. Or there is an absence of what might be called the neutrality reflex, the belief that the most intelligent response to possible conflict is to find ways not to fight. Or even more pertinently, where are our debates about the morality of war and the need to accept responsibility for what war brings? There seems to have been little acceptance of the idea that *unnecessary* wars incur a moral opprobrium not pertaining to wars that are just, and thereby inescapable. And for that matter, how many Australian leaders have ever given consideration to sentiments such as those of the 18th-century jurist Emmerich de Vattel, who, in discussion of the just causes of war, declared that a ruler who went to war was answerable for the attendant suffering of his own people, and was

> responsible also for all those [sufferings] which he inflicts upon an innocent people – the bloodshed, the pillaging of towns, the ruin of provinces – such are his crimes. Not a man is killed nor a hut burned but he is responsible before God and answerable to humanity for them.[9]

Two of Australia's wars a hundred years apart illustrate the point. In both the Boer War of 1899–1902 and the Second Gulf War of 2003–04, Australian contingents were sent to augment the forces of great and powerful friends. The justification used for both wars, in retrospect, turned out to be mendacious propaganda. Both involved particularly valuable resources – gold in the first case, oil in the second. Both were condemned in the wider world and both became a test of the great power's resolve. In each case the formal military campaigns were over quickly with the great power prevailing. The subsequent insurgency in Iraq and the guerrilla fighting on the veldt proved much harder to subdue. Both societies were ravaged, with utterly disproportionate civilian casualties. Atrocities and war crimes abounded – we still live with the disastrous aftermath of the Iraq war. In neither case did the Australian leaders suffer any opprobrium or face enquiries into their military adventurism. Nor was there any public expression of regret for the death and destruction. There was no sense of culpability, no acceptance of moral responsibility. Calls for a formal investigation into the circumstances of Australia's entry into the Iraq war have met with official silence. Australian governments find it easy to go to war. Their leaders seem to be able to withdraw with a calm conscience, answerable neither to God nor humanity.

When Australia celebrated the inauguration of the Commonwealth on the first day of the 20th century, the soldiers upstaged the statesmen. War was more glamorous than constitution-making. It was a portent. HB Higgins sensed that militarism threatened democracy, that war would eclipse the great achievement of establishing one of the world's most progressive democracies. He would find contemporary Australia troubling, for that is the implicit message of the carnival of commemoration supported by all the political parties and by many members of the community. The overriding theme is that the nation was made in conflict, that war was the defining experience and the digger the national exemplar. If that message holds, militarism will indeed have prevailed.

Notes

Abbreviations

AWM	Australian War Memorial
CPD	*Commonwealth Parliamentary Debates*
CUP	Cambridge University Press
n.d.	no date
NSWPD	*New South Wales Parliamentary Debates*
OUP	Oxford University Press
QPD	*Queensland Parliamentary Debates*
SAPD	*South Australian Parliamentary Debates*
VPD	*Victorian Parliamentary Debates*
WAPD	*Western Australian Parliamentary Debates*

Epigraphs

1 In J Morley, *The Life of Richard Cobden*, 13th edn, T Fisher Unwin, London, 1906, p. 638.

2 E de Vattel, *The Law of Nations or the Principles of Natural Law: Applied to the Conduct and to the Affairs of Nations and of Sovereigns*, trans. Charles G Fenwick, vol. 3, Oceana Publications, New York, 1964 (first published 1758), p. 243.

Introduction

1 See D Stephens, 'Why is Australia spending so much more on the Great War centenary than any other country?', John Menadue – Pearls and Irritations, 20 June 2015, <johnmenadue.com/blog/?p=4092>.

1 Unnecessary wars

1 Quoted in B Nicholson, 'We'll fight radical Islam for 100 years, says ex-army head Peter Leahy', *Weekend Australian*, 9–10 August 2014, <www.theaustralian.com.au/national-affairs/defence/well-fight-radical-islam-for-100-years-says-exarmy-head-peter-leahy/story-e6frg8yo-1227018630297?sv=b715945c949971df525a38e4d54dd45f>.

2 M Fraser, 'America: Australia's dangerous ally', *National Interest*, 12 January 2015, p. 2, <nationalinterest.org/feature/america-australias-dangerous-ally-11858>.

2 Australia's first birthday

1 The Commonwealth: celebrations in Rockhampton', *Morning Bulletin* (Rockhampton), 2 January 1901, p. 6.

2 'The birth of the Commonwealth: Hobart celebrations', *The Mercury* (Hobart), 1 January 1901, p. 3.

3 'The new century: a united Australia', *Kalgoorlie Miner*, 2 January 1901, p. 4.

4 'Commonwealth of Australia', *The Examiner* (Launceston), 2 January 1901, p. 4.

5 'Passing of the procession', *Sydney Morning Herald*, 2 January 1901, p. 10.

6 'Review of the military and naval forces', *Brisbane Courier*, 4 January 1901, p. 5.

7 'Demonstration at St. Mary's Cathedral' and 'A Commonwealth prayer', *Sydney Morning Herald*, 2 January 1901, pp. 9, 10–11.

8 'Troops for South Africa', *Sydney Morning Herald*, 8 January 1901, p. 4.

9 'Return of the Protector' and 'Welcome home again', *The Advertiser* (Adelaide), 7 January 1901, p. 4.

10 B Nicholls, *Bluejackets and Boxers: Australia's Naval Expedition to the Boxer Uprising*, Allen & Unwin, Sydney, 1986, pp. 90–1, 104–105.

11 'Passing of the procession', *Sydney Morning Herald*, 2 January 1901, p. 10.

12 'Reading of the proclamation', *West Australian*, 2 January 1901, p. 10.

13 'The procession', *The Queenslander*, 5 January 1901, p. 16.

14 'Hoisting the flag', *Morning Bulletin* (Rockhampton), 2 January 1901, p. 7.

15 JA La Nauze (ed.), *Federated Australia: Selections from Letters to the Morning Post 1900–1910*, Melbourne University Press, Melbourne, 1968, p. 26.

16 'The Commonwealth', *The Queenslander*, 5 January 1901, p. 8.

17 La Nauze (ed.), *Federated Australia*, p. 27.

18 'The army and volunteers', *Sydney Morning Herald*, 2 January 1901, p. 12.

19 *The Bulletin*, 12 January 1901.

20 HB Higgins, 'Australian ideals', *Austral Light*, 1 January 1902, pp. 15–16.

21 'In the other states', *The Argus*, 2 January 1901, p. 6.

22 'Message from the secretary of state for the colonies', *Sydney Morning Herald*, 2 January 1901, p. 11.

23 'The empire and federal honors', *The Advertiser* (Adelaide), 2 January 1901, p. 4.

24 *The Bulletin*, 28 September 1901.

3 Colonial defence: Australia or empire?

1 EA Freeman, *Greater Greece and Greater Britain*, Macmillan, London, 1886, p. 46.
2 'War with Russia', *The Empire*, 23 May 1854, p. 2.
3 JD Lang, *The Prospect for Australia in the Event of a War with France: Being a Lecture Delivered in Sydney in the Evening of Monday, August 23rd, 1858*, JL Sherriff, Sydney, 1858, pp. 4, 13.
4 JD Lang, *How to Defend the Colony*, JL Sherriff, Sydney, 1860, pp. iii, iv.
5 Lang, *The Prospect for Australia in the Event of a War with France*, p. 31.
6 Lang, *The Prospect for Australia in the Event of a War with France*, pp. 27, 28.
7 *VPD*, vol. 9, 10 November 1869, p. 2267.
8 *VPD*, vol. 9, 10 November 1869, p. 2185.
9 *VPD*, vol. 9, 10 November 1869, p. 2128.
10 *VPD*, vol. 9, 10 November 1869, pp. 2218–19.
11 *First Report of the Royal Commission ... upon the Necessity of a Federal Union ...*, Victorian Parliamentary Papers, 1870, 2nd Session, no. 10, p. 3.
12 *First Report of the Royal Commission*, p. 4.
13 Editorial, *The Age*, 10 October 1870, p. 2.
14 Editorial, *The Argus*, 7 October 1870, p. 4.
15 Editorial, *Sydney Morning Herald*, 11 October 1870, p. 4.
16 *NSWPD*, vol. 16, 18 March 1885, p. 77.
17 *NSWPD*, vol. 16, 18 March 1885, p. 118.
18 *NSWPD*, vol. 16, 24 March 1885, p. 233.
19 *NSWPD*, vol. 16, 17 March 1885, p. 56.
20 *NSWPD*, vol. 16, 18 March 1885, p. 103.
21 *NSWPD*, vol. 16, 20 March 1885, p. 162.
22 *NSWPD*, vol. 16, 19 March 1885, p. 159.
23 *NSWPD*, vol. 16, 20 March 1885, p. 181.
24 *NSWPD*, vol. 16, 18 March 1885, p. 105.
25 *NSWPD*, vol. 16, 17 March 1885, p. 39.
26 *NSWPD*, vol. 16, 18 March 1885, p. 107.
27 *NSWPD*, vol. 16, 19 March 1885, p. 133.
28 *NSWPD*, vol. 16, 19 March 1885, p. 127.
29 *NSWPD*, vol. 16, 20 March 1885, p. 179.
30 *NSWPD*, vol. 16, 19 March 1885, p. 121.
31 *NSWPD*, vol. 16, 18 March 1885, p. 62.
32 *VPD*, vol. 48, 17 June 1885, pp. 18–19.
33 *VPD*, vol. 48, 17 June 1885, p. 21.
34 *VPD*, vol. 48, 30 June and 2 July 1885, pp. 188, 246.
35 *VPD*, vol. 48, 25 June 1885, p. 145.
36 *VPD*, vol. 48, 24 June 1885, p. 130.
37 GN Griffiths, *NSWPD*, vol. 16, 24 March 1885, p. 211.
38 *NSWPD*, vol. 16, 20 March 1885, p. 193.

39 *NSWPD*, vol. 16, 20 March 1885, p. 197.
40 *NSWPD*, vol. 16, 19 March 1885, p. 138.
41 *NSWPD*, vol. 16, 18 March 1885, pp. 99–100.
42 *NSWPD*, vol. 16, 17 March 1885, pp. 24–6.
43 'The ceremony at the barracks', *Sydney Morning Herald*, 24 June 1885, p. 8.
44 'The ceremony at the barracks', *Sydney Morning Herald*, 24 June 1885, p. 8.
45 J Chamberlain, *Foreign and Colonial Speeches*, Routledge, London, 1897, p. 26.

4 Australia's radical patriots

1 G Salvemini, *Mazzini*, trans. IM Rawson, London, 1957, pp. 56–57.
2 J Morley, *The Life of Richard Cobden*, 13th edn, T Fisher Unwin, London, 1906, p. 109.
3 Morley, *The Life of Richard Cobden*, p. 230.
4 Morley, *The Life of Richard Cobden*, p. 230.
5 Morley, *The Life of Richard Cobden*, pp. 934–35.
6 JL Sturgis, *John Bright and Empire*, Athlone Press, London 1964, p. 184.
7 G Smith, *The Empire*, Henry & Parker, Oxford 1863, p. 36.
8 G Smith, *The Political Destiny of Canada*, Willig & Williamson, Toronto, 1878, p. 52.
9 Smith, *The Political Destiny of Canada*, p. 164.
10 Smith, *The Political Destiny of Canada*, p. 62.
11 Smith, *The Political Destiny of Canada*, p. 57.
12 Smith, *The Political Destiny of Canada*, p. 3.
13 JD Lang, *The Coming Event! Or Freedom and Independence for the Seven United Provinces of Australia*, Sampson Low, London, 1870, pp. vi, xi.
14 Lang, *The Coming Event!*, pp. 24–25, 32.
15 Lang, *The Coming Event!*, p. 84.
16 Lang, *The Coming Event!*, p. 68.
17 Lang, *The Coming Event!*, pp. 132–33.
18 Lang, *The Coming Event!*, p. 152.
19 R Hyslop, 'War scares in Australia in the 19th century', *Victorian Historical Journal*, vol. 47, no. 183, 1976, pp. 23–44.
20 Hyslop, 'War scares in Australia in the 19th century', p. 38.
21 *QPD*, vol. 53, 17 and 22 November 1887, pp. 1634, 1718.
22 *QPD*, vol. 53, 22 November 1887, p. 1703.
23 *QPD*, vol. 53, 17 November 1887, pp. 1633–34.
24 *QPD*, vol. 53, 17 November 1887, p. 1635.
25 *QPD*, vol. 53, 22 November 1887, p. 1705.
26 *NSWPD*, vol. 29, 25 November 1887, p. 1606.
27 *NSWPD*, vol. 29, 24 November 1887, p. 1571.
28 *NSWPD*, vol. 29, 24 November 1887, pp. 1570, 1572–73.
29 M McKenna, *The Captive Republic: A History of Republicanism in Australia, 1788–1996*, CUP, Cambridge, 1996, pp. 121–22, 151.
30 'The premier's banquet', *Sydney Morning Herald*, 7 February 1890, p. 8.
31 J Hirst, *The Sentimental Nation*, OUP, Melbourne, 2000, p. 11.
32 FM Neasey, *Andrew Inglis Clark*, University of Tasmania Law Press,

Hobart, 2001, p. 116.
33 N Gangulee (ed.), *Giuseppe Mazzini: Selected Writings*, LD Limited, London, n.d., p. 130.
34 W Jethro Brown, *Why Federate? A Paper Read before the Australasian Association for the Advancement of Science*, Angus & Robertson, Sydney, 1898, p. 37.
35 R Ely (ed.), *A Living Force: Andrew Inglis Clark and the Ideal of Commonwealth*, Centre for Tasmanian Historical Studies, Hobart, 2001, p. 199.
36 *Proceedings and Debates of the Australian Federation Conference, Melbourne, 1890*, Government Printer, Melbourne, 1890, p. 36.
37 *The Quadrilateral*, 1874, p. 109.
38 *The Quadrilateral*, 1874, p. 57.
39 AI Clark, 'The evils of monarchy', unpublished manuscript, Clark papers, C4/F4, University of Tasmania Archives.
40 BR Wise, *The Making of the Australian Commonwealth*, Longman, London, 1913, p. 75.
41 Letter, G Higinbotham to AI Clark, 8 March 1891, Clark papers, C4/C206, University of Tasmania Archives.
42 'The appellate provisions of the Constitution of the Commonwealth of Australia', *Sydney Morning Herald*, 2 August 1900, p. 4.
43 'The appellate provisions of the Constitution of the Commonwealth of Australia', *Sydney Morning Herald*, 2 August 1900, p. 4.
44 A Deakin, *Imperial Federation: An Address Delivered by the Hon. Alfred Deakin, M.P. at the Annual Meeting of the Imperial Federation League of Victoria, Town Hall, Melbourne, June 14, 1905*, Echo Publishing Co., Melbourne, 1905, p. 6.
45 Editorial, *The Empire*, 10 October 1870, p. 2.

5 The appeal of sceptre and crown

1 JA Froude, 'England and her colonies', *Fraser's Magazine*, January 1870, p. 17.
2 TE Kebbel (ed.), *Selected Speeches of the Earl of Beaconsfield*, vol. 2, Longman, Green and Co., London, 1882, p. 530.
3 WE Forster, *Imperial Federation*, Kegan Paul, French and Co., London, 1885, p. 2.
4 A Patchett Martin, *Australia and the Empire*, David Douglas, Edinburgh, 1889, p. 210.
5 JA Froude, *Oceana, Or, England and Her Colonies*, Longman, Green and Co., London, 1886, p. 174.
6 JR Seeley, *The Expansion of England*, Macmillan, London, 1916 (first published 1883), pp. 350, 346.
7 CS Blackton, 'Australian nationality and nationalism: the imperial federation interlude, 1885–1901', *Historical Studies - Australia and New Zealand*, vol. 7, no. 25, November 1955, p. 7.
8 Blackton, 'Australian nationality and nationalism', p. 6.
9 'National unity: address by Mr. G.R. Parkin', *Sydney Morning Herald*,

19 June 1889, p. 4.
10 'National unity: address by Mr. G.R. Parkin', *Sydney Morning Herald*, 19 June 1889, p. 4.
11 'Imperial federation', *Tasmanian News*, 25 April 1888, p. 2.
12 HG Turner, 'Australia militant', *Melbourne Review*, vol. 10, 1885, pp. 143–44, 153.
13 R Thomson, *Australian Nationalism: An Earnest Appeal to the Sons of Australia in Favour of the Federation and Independence of the States of Our Country*, Moss Brothers, Sydney, 1888, pp. 76–77, 81.
14 GD Meudell, 'An Australian protest against imperial federation', *Melbourne Review*, vol. 10, 1885, p. 249.
15 DG Ferguson, 'The future of the Australian colonies', *Centennial Magazine*, vol. 1, no. 11, June 1889, p. 763.
16 Meudell, 'An Australian protest against imperial federation', p. 250.
17 Letter, CW Dilke to his father, 4 June 1867, 'Letters of Sir Charles Dilke and Alfred Deakin, 1866–1910', National Library of Australia, microfilm, Mfm G 28412.
18 Letter, CW Dilke to his father, 3 March 1867.
19 CW Dilke, *Greater Britain: A Record of Travel in English-speaking Countries During 1866–7*, 8th edn, Macmillan, London, 1885 (first published 1868), p. vii.
20 See D Bell, *The Idea of Greater Britain*, Princeton University Press, Princeton, New Jersey, 2007, p. 9.
21 G Varouxakis, *Mill on Nationality*, Routledge, London, 2002, p. 134.
22 Bell, *The Idea of Greater Britain*, p. 63.
23 Bell, *The Idea of Greater Britain*, p. 117.
24 Seeley, *The Expansion of England*, p. 346.
25 Cited in Bell, *The Idea of Greater Britain*, p. 9.
26 Cited in HE Egerton, *The British Dominions and the War*, OUP, London, 1914, p. 8.
27 Froude, 'England and her colonies', p. 1.
28 JM MacKenzie, *Propaganda and Empire: The Manipulation of British Public Opinion, 1880–1960*, Manchester University Press, Manchester, 1984.
29 G Parkin, *Imperial Federation, the Problem of National Unity*, Macmillan, London, 1892, p. 3.
30 Seeley, *The Expansion of England*, p. iv.
31 CW Oman, *England in the Nineteenth Century*, Edward Arnold, London, pp. 258–61.
32 WJ Sowden, *An Australian Native's Viewpoint*, Macmillan, London, 1912, p. 6.
33 CS Blackton, 'Australian nationality and nativism: the Australian Natives' Association, 1885–1901', *Journal of Modern History*, vol. 30, no. 1, March 1958, p. 39.
34 A Deakin, *Imperial Federation: An Address Delivered by the Hon. Alfred Deakin, M.P. at the Annual Meeting of the Imperial Federation League of Victoria, Town Hall, Melbourne, June 14, 1905*, Echo Publishing Co., Melbourne, 1905, pp. 6–7.

35 EA Freeman, *Greater Greece and Greater Britain*, Macmillan, London, 1886, p. 46; see chapter 3 in this book.
36 JA Hobson, *The Crisis of Liberalism: New Issues of Democracy*, PS King & Son, London, 1909, p. 242.

6 The illusions of an imperial family

1 Cited in D Bell, *The Idea of Greater Britain*, Princeton University Press, Princeton, New Jersey, 2007, p. 45.
2 Both Rosebery and Grey cited in HCG Matthew, *The Liberal Imperialists: The Ideas and Politics of a Post-Gladstonian Élite*, OUP, Oxford, 1973, p. 162.
3 CW Boyd (ed.), *Mr Chamberlain's Speeches*, vol. 1, Constable, London, 1914, p. 278.
4 A Hasluck (ed.), *Audrey Tennyson's Vice-Regal Days*, National Library of Australia, Canberra, 1978, p. 102.
5 Letter, I Hamilton to his wife, Adelaide, 5 January 1914, Hamilton Papers, 5/1/76, King's College, London.
6 AG Austin (ed.), *The Webbs' Australian Diary 1898*, Sir Isaac Pitman & Sons, Melbourne, 1965, p. 108.
7 D Cannadine, *Ornamentalism: How the British Saw Their Empire*, OUP, Oxford, 2001, pp. 124–25.
8 R Hyam, *Elgin and Churchill at the Colonial Office, 1905–1908*, Macmillan, London, 1968, p. 318.
9 R Hyam, *Britain's Imperial Century, 1815–1914*, Macmillan, London, 1976, p. 237.
10 Cited in N d'Ombrain, *War Machinery and High Policy*, OUP, London, 1973, p. 229.
11 Cited in JE Kendle, *Colonial and Imperial Conferences, 1887–1911*, London, 1967, p. 225.
12 GM Trevelyan, *Grey of Fallodon*, Longman Green, London, 1935, p. 153.
13 Cited in Hyam, *Elgin and Churchill at the Colonial Office, 1905–1908*, p. 318.
14 LT Hobhouse, *Democracy and Reaction*, Harvester Press, Brighton, 1972 (first published 1904), p. 23.
15 Kendle, *Colonial and Imperial Conferences*, p. 226.
16 D Day, *The Politics of War*, HarperCollins, Sydney, 2003, p. 237.
17 Letter, CW Dilke to his father, 4 June 1867, 'Letters of Sir Charles Dilke and Alfred Deakin, 1866–1910', National Library of Australia, microfilm, Mfm G 28412.
18 SA Froude, *Oceana, Or, England and Her Colonies*, Longman, Green and Co., London, 1886, pp. 298–99.
19 Hyam, *Britain's Imperial Century*, p. 334.
20 I Hamilton, *Compulsory Service*, John Murray, London, 1910, p. 121.
21 E Hutton, 'The bond of military unity', in CS Goldman (ed.), *The Empire and the Century*, John Murray, London, 1905, p. 232.
22 WEH Lecky, *The Empire: Its Value and its Growth*, Longman Green, London, 1893, pp. 18–19.
23 J Chamberlain, *Foreign and Colonial Speeches*, Routledge, London, 1897, p. 27.

24 Froude, *Oceana*, p. 174; see chapter 5 in this book.
25 CW Dilke, *The British Empire*, Chatto & Windus, London, 1899, p. 1.
26 CW Dilke & S Wilkinson, *Imperial Defence*, Macmillan, London, 1892, pp. 233–34.
27 Dilke, *The British Empire*, pp. 12, 139.
28 CW Dilke, *Greater Britain: A Record of Travel in English-speaking Countries During 1866–7*, 8th edn, Macmillan, London, 1885 (first published 1868), p. 12.
29 Dilke & Wilkinson, *Imperial Defence*, p. 37.
30 Dilke, *The British Empire*, p. 11.
31 Chamberlain, *Foreign and Colonial Speeches*, p. 77.
32 CW Boyd (ed.), *Mr. Chamberlain's Speeches*, vol. 2, Constable, London, 1914, p. 4. The Temple of Janus, an allusion well known to a classically educated audience, stood in the Roman Forum. Its two doors were opened in times of war and closed in times of peace.
33 JL Garvin, *The Life of Joseph Chamberlain*, vol. 3, 1895–1900, Macmillan, London, p. 476.
34 'The secretary for war on colonial loyalty', *Sydney Morning Herald*, 4 November 1899, p. 9.
35 Colonial Office, NSW Despatches and Correspondence on Offices and Individuals, UK National Archives, CO 201/625, 1899, no. 24346.
36 JA Hobson, *The Psychology of Jingoism*, Grant Richards, London, 1901, p. 42.
37 Boyd (ed.), *Mr. Chamberlain's Speeches*, vol. 2, pp. 70–71, 72.
38 Cited in Matthew, *The Liberal Imperialists*, p. 162.
39 JF Owen, 'The military forces of our colonies', *Fortnightly Review*, no. 1, 1900, p. 493.
40 AC Doyle, *The Great Boer War*, George Bell, London, 1902, pp. 742–43.

7 Australia's soldiers of the Queen

1 'The farewell parade', *The Argus*, 30 October 1899, p. 4.
2 'The farewell parade', *The Argus*, 30 October 1899, p. 4.
3 'General news', *The Advertiser* (Adelaide), 1 November 1899, p. 4.
4 'The demonstration at Circular Quay', *Sydney Morning Herald*, 4 November 1899, p. 9.
5 'Farewell to the contingent', *The Argus*, 28 October 1899, p. 13.
6 'The municipal entertainment', *Sydney Morning Herald*, 14 November 1899, p. 5.
7 'Patriotic fund meeting', *Sydney Morning Herald*, 3 November 1899, p. 5.
8 Beauchamp, secret telegram to J Chamberlain, 24 October 1899, Colonial Office: NSW Despatches and Correspondence on Offices and Individuals, UK National Archives, CO201/265, 1899, no. 29489.
9 'Queensland contingent: message from the Queen', *The Queenslander*, 4 November 1899, p. 888.
10 *QPD*, vol. 82, no. 2, 11 October 1899, pp. 339, 341.
11 'The Transvaal contingent: a variety of opinions', *The Mercury* (Hobart), 11 October 1899, p. 4.
12 'Parliament', *The Argus*, 12 October 1899, p. 3.

13 WK Hancock, *Australia*, Jacaranda, Brisbane, 1964 (first published 1930), p. 49.
14 *CPD*, vol. 7, 14 January 1902, p. 8798.
15 *CPD*, vol. 14, 16 July 1903, p. 2265.
16 *WAPD*, vol. 14, 5 October 1899, pp. 1556, 1558.
17 *NSWPD*, vol. 100, 19 October 1899, p. 1495.
18 *CPD*, vol. 7, 29 January 1902, p. 9385.
19 *NSWPD*, vol. 100, 19 October 1899, p. 1496.
20 *CPD*, vol. 18, 18 March 1904, p. 735.
21 *CPD*, vol. 7, 14 January 1902, p. 8747.
22 *NSWPD*, vol. 2, 25 July 1900, p. 1284.
23 *NSWPD*, vol. 2, 25 July 1900, p. 1299.
24 'The relief of Kimberley', *The Advertiser* (Adelaide), 20 February 1900, p. 5.
25 'Relief of Ladysmith: how Hobart took the news', *The Mercury* (Hobart), 3 March 1900, p. 5.
26 'The relief of Ladysmith: enthusiastic demonstration in Melbourne', *Sydney Morning Herald*, 5 March 1900, p. 8.
27 'Great popular demonstration', *Sydney Morning Herald*, 21 May 1900, p. 8.
28 'The celebrations in Hobart', *The Mercury* (Hobart), 21 May 1900, p. 3.
29 'Great popular demonstration', *Sydney Morning Herald*, 21 May 1900, p. 7.
30 'The celebrations in Hobart', *The Mercury* (Hobart), 21 May 1900, p. 3.
31 'Great popular demonstration', *Sydney Morning Herald*, 21 May 1900, p. 8.
32 'Celebrations in the country', *Sydney Morning Herald*, 22 May 1900, p. 6.

8 The critics of the war

1 *NSWPD*, vol. 2, 25 July 1900, p. 1297.
2 *SAPD*, 10 October 1899, p. 639.
3 *QPD*, vol. 82, no. 2, 11 October 1899, p. 350
4 *QPD*, vol. 82, no. 2, 12 October 1899, p. 389.
5 *WAPD*, vol. 14, 5 October 1899, p. 1559.
6 *QPD*, vol. 82, no. 2, 17 October 1899, p. 416.
7 *SAPD*, 10 October 1899, p. 148.
8 *NSWPD*, vol. 2, 19 October 1899, p. 1555.
9 *NSWPD*, vol. 2, 25 July 1900, p. 1297.
10 *VPD*, vol. 92, 10 October 1899, p. 1734.
11 *VPD*, vol. 92, 10 October 1899, p. 1768.
12 *VPD*, vol. 92, 10 October 1899, p. 1746.
13 *SAPD*, 10 October 1899, p. 628.
14 *QPD*, vol. 82, no. 2, 11 October 1899, p. 351.
15 *VPD*, vol. 92, 10 October 1899, p. 1751.
16 *QPD*, vol. 82, no. 2, 18 October 1899, p. 452.
17 *QPD*, vol. 82, no. 2, 17 October 1899, p. 416.
18 *NSWPD*, vol. 2, 25 July 1900, p. 1288.
19 *QPD*, vol. 82, no. 2, 18 October 1899, p. 453.
20 *CPD*, vol. 3, 24 July 1901, p. 2990.
21 *CPD*, vol. 7, 14 January 1902, pp. 8757, 8758.
22 *VPD*, vol. 92, 10 October 1899, p. 1777.

23 *CPD*, vol. 7, 14 January 1902, p. 8754.
24 *CPD*, vol. 7, 14 January 1902, p. 8758.
25 HB Higgins, *The Duties of Patriotism*, Advocate Printing Works, Melbourne, 1902, p. 13.
26 JB Higgins, 'Australian ideals', *Austral Light*, 1 January 1902, p. 15.
27 CI Clark, 'Early life and antecedents of A.I. Clark', unpublished manuscript, SD_ILS:550831, Crowther collection, State Library of Tasmania.
28 Cited in JA Allen, *Rose Scott: Vision and Revision in Feminism*, OUP, Melbourne, 1994, p. 150.
29 'To our readers', *The Dawn*, 1 December 1899, p. 7.
30 *Daily Telegraph* (Sydney), 10 October 1899.
31 *Daily Telegraph* (Sydney), 11 November 1899.
32 *Daily Telegraph* (Sydney), 10 December 1901.
33 JA La Nauze (ed.), *Federated Australia: An Address Delivered by the Hon. Alfred Deakin, M.P. at the Annual Meeting of the Imperial Federation League of Victoria, Town Hall, Melbourne, June 14, 1905*, Echo Publishing Co., Melbourne, 1905, pp. 101–102.
34 *NSWPD*, vol. 2, 19 October 1899, p. 1506–507.
35 *CPD*, vol. 7, 14 January 1902, p. 8800.
36 *CPD*, vol. 7, 14 January 1902, pp. 8748–49.
37 *CPD*, vol. 7, 22 January 1902, pp. 9018, 9026.
38 *The Bulletin*, 21 October 1899.
39 *The Bulletin*, 28 October 1899.
40 *The Bulletin*, 23 December 1899.
41 *The Bulletin*, 6 January 1900.
42 *The Bulletin*, 6 January 1900.
43 *The Bulletin*, 29 March 1902.
44 *The Bulletin*, 29 March 1902.
45 *The Bulletin*, 29 March 1902.
46 *Tocsin*, 19 October 1899.
47 *Tocsin*, 2 November 1899.
48 *Tocsin*, 18 January 1900.
49 *Tocsin*, 5 July 1900.
50 The expression of the Rev. DR Strong, *Tocsin*, 13 September 1900.
51 *Tocsin*, 17 January 1901.
52 *Tocsin*, 23 August 1900.
53 *The Worker*, 6 July 1901.
54 *The Worker*, 24 May 1902.

9 Involvement in an infamous war

1 CP Lucas, *Greater Rome and Greater Britain*, Clarendon Press, Oxford, 1912, p. 174.
2 CW Dilke, *Greater Britain: A Record of Travel in English-speaking Countries During 1866–7*, 8th edn, Macmillan, London, 1885 (first published 1868), p. 152.
3 *CPD*, vol. 18, 18 March 1904, pp. 726, 728.

4 A Haultain (ed.), *A Selection from Goldwin Smith's Correspondence*, T Werner Laurie, London, 1911, p. 350.
5 See WJ Mommsen, 'Introduction', in K Wilson (ed.), *The International Impact of the Boer War*, Palgrave, New York, 2001, p. 1.
6 Mommsen, 'Introduction', in Wilson (ed.), *The International Impact of the Boer War*, p. 1.
7 LT Hobhouse, *Democracy and Reaction*, Harvester Press, Brighton, 1972 (first published 1904), p. 28.
8 'T.' (PS Reinsch), *An American View of the South African Situation*, Ernest Temple Hargrove, New York, 1901, pp. 4–5.
9 LT Hobhouse, *Democracy and Reaction*, Harvester Press, Brighton, 1972 (first published 1904), p. 142.
10 RWF Droogleever (ed.), *From the Front: A.B. Paterson's Dispatches from the Boer War*, Macmillan, Sydney, 2000, pp. 127–28.
11 P Lewson (ed.), *Selections from the Correspondence of John X Merriman*, vol. 3, 1899–1905, Van Riebeeck Society, Cape Town, 1966, pp. 84, 111, 150.
12 Lewson (ed.), *Selections from the Correspondence of John X Merriman*, p. 336.
13 Lewson (ed.), *Selections from the Correspondence of John X Merriman*, pp. 139–42.
14 P Warwick, *The South African War*, Longman, London, 1980, p. 130.
15 AB Downes, *Targeting Civilians in War*, Cornell University Press, Ithaca, New York, 2008, p. 109.
16 P Warwick, *Black People and the South African War, 1899–1902*, CUP, Cambridge, 1983, p. 4; SB Spies, *Methods of Barbarism? Roberts and Kitchener and Civilians in the Boer Republics, January 1900 – May 1902*, Human & Rousseau, Cape Town, 1977, pp. 262–65.
17 B Nasson, 'South Africa's post-Boer Boer War', in P Dennis & J Grey (eds), *The Boer War: Army, Nation, Empire*, Department of Defence, Canberra, 2000, p. 14.
18 Lewson (ed.), *Selections from the Correspondence of John X. Merriman*, p. 463.
19 Cited in Spies, *Methods of Barbarism*, p. 297.
20 'A pro-Boer meeting at Savernake', *Sydney Morning Herald*, 1 January 1902, p. 7. I am indebted to Justin Moloney for referring me to this report.
21 J Bufton, *Tasmanians in the Transvaal War*, SG Loone, Hobart, 1905, p. 370.
22 Bufton, *Tasmanians in the Transvaal War*, pp. 140–44.
23 Bufton, *Tasmanians in the Transvaal War*, pp. 224, 227, 228, 230, 288, 293, 307, 308, 323, 360.
24 Bufton, *Tasmanians in the Transvaal War*, p. 361.
25 Bufton, *Tasmanians in the Transvaal War*, p. 306.
26 Bufton, *Tasmanians in the Transvaal War*, p. 212.
27 Bufton, *Tasmanians in the Transvaal War*, pp. 379–80.
28 Bufton, *Tasmanians in the Transvaal War*, p. 170.
29 C Wilcox, 'Looking back on the South African War', in Dennis & Grey (eds), *The Boer War*, pp. 10–11.
30 RS Skirving, *Our Army in South Africa*, Angus & Robertson, Sydney, 1901, p. 15.

31 *CPD*, vol. 18, 17 March 1904, pp. 718–19.
32 *CPD*, vol. 18, 19 November 1904, p. 784.

10 The nation's selective memory

1 C Wilcox, *Australia's Boer War: The War in South Africa, 1899–1902*, AWM & OUP, Melbourne, 2002.
2 Wilcox, *Australia's Boer War*, p. 359.
3 *Herald Sun*, 18 December 2012.
4 '2014 50c Boer War coin', Royal Australian Mint eshop, <eshop.ramint.gov.au/2014-50c-Boer-War-Coin/310324.aspx>.
5 Department of Defence, 27 May 2002, <www.defence.gov.au/minister/15tpl.cfm?CurrentId=1539>.
6 P Cosgrove, 'Message for Boer War Day 2015', Boer War Memorial Association, <www.bwm.org.au/documents/GGMessageBWD2015.pdf>.
7 MD Binskin, 'A Message from the chief of the Defence Force', Boer War Memorial Association, <www.bwm.org.au/documents/2015CDF.pdf>.
8 A Abbott, 'A message from the prime minister', Boer War Memorial Association, <www.bwm.org.au/documents/2014_PM_BWD.pdf>.
9 G Blainey, 'Foreword', in Wilcox, *Australia's Boer War*, p. v.
10 'The Boer War', Australian Government, <www.australia.gov.au/about-australia/Australian-story/boer-war>.
11 Wilcox, *Australia's Boer War*, p. 345.
12 Wilcox, *Australia's Boer War*, p. 347.
13 Wilcox, *Australia's Boer War*, p. 346.
14 'The Boer War', Australian Government, <www.australia.gov.au/about-australia/Australian-story/boer-war>.
15 WT Reay, *Australians in War*, Massina & Co., Melbourne, 1900, pp. 6, 11.
16 Reay, 'Introduction', *Australians in War*, p. 7.
17 Press release, 'Memorial director encourages all Australians to support veterans of current and recent conflicts this Anzac Day', AWM, 10 April 2013, <www.awm.gov.au/media/releases/memorial-director-encourages-all-australians-support-veterans-current-and-recent>.
18 J Brown, 'Was the war in Afghanistan worth it?', *Sydney Morning Herald*, 1 January 2015, <www.smh.com.au/comment/was-the-war-in-afghanistan-worth-it-20141230-12fx1l.html>.
19 D Wroe, 'War footing: minister eyes next hotspot', *Sydney Morning Herald*, 21–22 September 2013, <www.smh.com.au/national/war-footing-minister-eyes-next-hotspot-20130920-2u5dm.html>.
20 R Lowell, 'Waking early Sunday morning', 1965, in *Collected Poems*, Farrar, Straus and Giroux, New York, 2007.

11 Dangerous allies or great and powerful friends?

1 D Stephens, 'Why is Australia spending so much more on the Great War centenary than any other country?', John Menadue, 'Pearls and irritations', 20 June 2015, <johnmenadue.com/blog/?p=4092>.
2 See D Martin, *Armed Neutrality for Australia*, Dove, Melbourne, 1984; D Martin, 'Armed neutrality', in M Teichmann (ed.), *Aspects of Australian*

Defence, Monash University, Melbourne, 1966, pp. 77–88.

3 Martin, 'Armed neutrality', p. 80.

4 Martin, 'Armed neutrality', p. 81.

5 Martin, 'Armed neutrality', p. 78.

6 M Fraser, *Dangerous Allies*, Melbourne University Press, Melbourne, 2015; M Fraser, 'America: Australia's dangerous ally', *National Interest*, January–February 2015; M Fraser, 'Letting go of the US', *The Age*, 26 August, 2013; M Fraser, 'Our star-spangled manner', *The Age*, 7 June 2012.

7 M Fraser, 'We no longer have a capacity to stay out of America's wars', John Menadue, 'Pearls and irritations', 7 Aug 2015, <johnmenadue.com/blog/?p=4335>.

8 See P Stanley, *Invading Australia: Japan and the Battle for Australia*, Viking, Melbourne, 2008.

9 E de Vattel, *The Law of Nations or the Principles of Natural Law: Applied to the Conduct and to the Affairs of Nations and of Sovereigns*, trans. Charles G Fenwick, vol. 3, Oceana Publications, New York, 1964 (first published 1758), p. 243.

Acknowledgments

Where to begin, I wonder? A book is likely to be a meeting point of innumerable ideas and influences. And in this case it has been about a year in the making, while the topic in question – Australia's place in the world – has been of interest and, often enough, concern to me for much of my adult life. Although I have written about many specific aspects of the past, I taught general courses in Australian history and politics for many years. There will inevitably be echoes of the work of scholars whose books I have forgotten, whose ideas were recorded in notes and lectures I no longer have.

More immediately, I must acknowledge the tolerance and patience of family and friends who put up with my periodic preoccupation, which verged on obsession while the text was taking shape. Like any non-fiction writer, I owe a debt to many libraries and archives. I should mention in particular the National Library of Australia and the great public libraries in Melbourne and Sydney, with their collections of books from the 19th and early 20th centuries. I have been fortunate in my choice of publisher: NewSouth Publishing. I appreciated the exuberant enthusiasm of Phillipa McGuinness and the exemplary, sharp-eyed editing of Nicola Young.

There are numerous writers whose work I read with appreciation while the book was taking shape. I am thinking of, among others, the late Malcolm Fraser, Peter Stanley, Hugh White, Stephen Fitzgerald, David Day and Douglas Newton.

Like other books of mine, this one grew out of earlier works, and in this case two in particular: *Drawing the Global Colour Line* (2008), co-authored with Marilyn Lake; and *What's Wrong with Anzac?* (2010) written with her, Mark McKenna and Joy Damousi. I owe a particular debt to Marilyn. During the period we collaborated on these two books, we discussed and argued fruitfully about many of the themes that are now woven through the texture of *Unnecessary Wars*.

Index

Index

MIX
Papier | Fördert gute Waldnutzung
FSC® C083411

Zeitfracht Medien GmbH
Ferdinand-Jühlke-Straße 7
99095 Erfurt, Deutschland
produktsicherheit@kolibri360.de